THE LINCOLN

GORDON JACKSON

THE LINCOLN PSALTER

Versions of the Psalms

Afterword by Donald Davie

CARCANET

First published in 1997 by
Carcanet Press Limited
4th Floor, Conavon Court
12–16 Blackfriars Street
Manchester M3 5BQ

A CIP catalogue record for this book
is available from the British Library
ISBN 1 85754 265 7

The publisher acknowledges financial assistance
from the Arts Council of England

Set in Sabon by CentraCet Ltd, Cambridge
Printed and bound in England by SRP Ltd, Exeter

for Donald Davie

He taught me a new song,
gave me a new kind of singing,
a new way of praising God.

Psalm 40

Preface

The ancient Hebrew anthology known as *Tehillim* or 'Praises' has a coherence more apparent than real. Any translator confers upon the material the single stamp of his age and language and purpose, and so clouds the diversity of style and period of his ultimate sources. Even so, there is in the collection a coherence not so much of style but of content: the ancient writers said what they had to say within a tradition that itself came from the pattern of human needs, and it is that tradition that makes the psalms still valuable to us. We still live in circumstances where the wicked prosper, where God seemingly tolerates insult, where injustice and despair are all about us. God who should be stepping in to right wrongs is *absconditus*, somewhere in hiding; we know he is going to act, but why is he so long about it; will he be too late, at least for me.

That has always been the starting point of desperate prayer. The rest of praying is a rhetoric of arm-twisting and pleading, flattering and reminding, vowing and promising. It's why we don't need to know who the psalmist is; we already know his inner self because we share his need, his anguish, his hope, and his delight; we know him because he is us.

In this sense we might say that the psalms are less dependent than any other kind of poetry on 'accurate' or 'sensitive' translation. The very worst versions may readily speak to our condition. We use them. We regard them as aids to prayer and praise. After so many centuries and shifts in religion, they are still functional.

But the psalms are still poems, and a poem has not only a social function but also an artistic essence. And the essence of an ancient poem has continually to be searched for because fashion changes and translations date; and the more valuable a text is, the more we have need of successive versions of it.

When Miles Coverdale died in 1568 he could have had little reason to believe his Psalter would be revered across the whole globe nearly five hundred years later. In his own lifetime translations of the scriptures were pouring from the presses, and his own first complete Bible in English he viewed as an amateur work based on other translations in German and Latin and Tyndale's English, and without the advantage of Hebrew or Greek. And yet his version of the Psalter is still sung in Anglican cathedral choirs as the most normal libretto, and even said daily in cathedral chapters in its entirety. To many it is the psalms in the truest English, and stands side by side with Shakespeare in celebrating the particular power and glory of the English tongue. It is a national monument, a heritage to enjoy and to pass on undiminished. To such as love the translator who tells us

> God is gone up with a merry noise,
>> and the lord with the sound of the trump

any new version of the psalms will be stilted and dull; they will not allow anyone to equal the dignity of

> Deliver my soul from the sword,
>> my darling from the power of the dog.

And why should they? Coverdale has invented a medium that can contain energy and dignity; it can speak and it can sing. Why should any try to supersede it?

They don't, of course. Other versions do other things, and there's plenty of room for more. Partly from age and partly from respect, Coverdale's version tends to look venerable. Like a medieval cathedral, no one wants to 'improve' it; no one would think nowadays of replacing it; yet most medieval buildings we revere are a mixture of fashions and additions that the tarnish of age has unified for us. The psalms in the Book of Common Prayer have an antique delight for us that was not there for Coverdale or Cranmer. They were composed in contemporary English, modern and colloquial and a far cry from the 'traditional' Latin they replaced. When Coverdale writes

> Tush say they, how should God perceive it,
>> is there knowledge in the Most High?

we perhaps hear the voice of Shakespeare's Iago or Richard III, but Tudor readers would hear the man in the tavern, the woman in the street.

The version of the Psalter I present here, then, is not so much a replacement of Coverdale (that would be impossible), but a homage to it. It is an attempt to recreate in some measure what Coverdale has achieved, namely a version of the psalms that invites us not only to enter into them ourselves, but also to drag in with us the contemporary world in which we live. We must find room for the tyrants and oppressors of our time along with David's adversaries, and use his circumstances to make sense of ours. Which is, in short, the work of the poem.

This is not, then, a 'colloquial' version; it makes use of colloquial language as Coverdale's did, and as the originals no doubt did, because the psalm is the voice of speaking man, a mortal addressing an Immortal through a medium they share. But these versions with their archaic furniture of breastplates, arrows and mountain fortifications are as much antique as contemporary. I have easily resisted the temptation to update everything and make a *psalms for modern man*. That would be to omit the fact that what we call the psalms includes three thousand years of theological patina which can not be removed. My practice, therefore, has been to employ Pound's palimpsest approach, leaving the elders of Israel, the medieval crusaders, the bishops and reformers and the old pious prophetesses in the pews to get on with each other as well as they may. The readers of the psalms, the praise-givers, are a kingdom not a party, and it's good that we see them all together there. Where my props of the moment appear I hope they do not wrest attention to themselves; they are, after all, only temporarily up-to-date.

The other main feature of my method, insofar as I have one, is the quest for the poem. Most translators of the scriptures are quite rightly concerned with searching for the text, what the putative original actually says. How it says it has generally been a secondary concern. Even the medium of the writing has been traditionally unconsidered, resulting in a compromise of apparently prose lines in numbered 'verses'. More recent versions in this century have sought to show that some parts of the Bible are poetic by using sculpted verses, a practice in layout which is perhaps only as recent as printing itself.

I have tried to follow the structural features as well as I could. I have followed Knox in the acrostic psalms, reducing the 26 characters of the English alphabet to the 22 of the Hebrew by missing out the problematic ones (eight lines starting with x or z would have forced me to abandon the strategy, and possibly Knox as well). And I have not numbered the verses, but I have tried to follow the patterns of parallel thought and statement. Thereafter the business has been much a matter of observing the similitudes, and establishing a sort of rhythmic integrity.

The literal translator sooner or later comes up against a passage that seems to make little sense. The more he clings to the sense his scholarship tells him is true, the less sense it seems to make. Young for example, in his *Literal Translation of the Bible*, gives us for Psalm 58:9:

> Before your pots discern the bramble
> As well the raw as the heated He whirleth away.

This adds a riddle to the text which probably was not in the 'original': what's raw and heated and whirleth away?

Peter Levi, in the Penguin *Psalms*, gives us the less confused:

> · Quicker than the pot can feel the heat,
> quicker than the fresh thorn withers,
> the tempest shall carry them away.

I admit I know little of the speed of withering thorns, but if that is a measure of a tempest's fury I must know less than I thought I did.

The New English Bible makes the image at least consistent:

> All unawares, may they be rooted up like a thorn-bush,
> like weeds which a man angrily clears away!

That doesn't sound too bad, till you give thought to that violent gardener who must have had a row with his wife and is determined to take it out on the nearest untidy thorn-bush. My own small experience of eradicating knotty thorn-bushes, however, leads me to consider the task a good afternoon's work, and certainly not the sort of thing to do in a huff.

Monsignor Ronald Knox, whose work I have followed more closely than most others, seems less inspired over this verse:

> Green stalks the whirlwind carries away,
> while yonder pot still waits for fuel!

But what is the pot doing there at all, and why do we need to sympathise with its inconvenience? In Homer it might be a splendid marginal detail, but that's not the sort of thing Hebrew poetry is made of. I think his cold pot is a red herring.

Coverdale gives us, as usual, the goods:

> Or ever your pots be made hot with thorns:
> so let indignation vex him, even as a thing that is raw.

The vexation, the wicked man's or else God's, is likened to fire put to the cooking pot. Presumably the thing that is raw is, or ought to be for the sense's sake, the wicked man, like a skinless sausage falling into hot water. Coverdale isn't usually so squeamish as to pass off a concrete detail as some vague guess in translationese, 'a thing that is raw.' He must have been in some doubt when he cooked up that phrase or else more innocent of cooking than any man ever.

The AV starts confidently enough:

10

> Before your pots can feel the thorns, he shall take them away
> as with a whirlwind,

which is well on track, but then comes 'both living, and in his wrath' and we're back in viruswrite.

David Frost in the ASB's *Liturgical Psalter* does better than any:

> Before they know it let them be cut down like thorns:
> like brambles which a man sweeps angrily aside.

That's consistent; the gardener energetically cuts down briars and rakes them aside, and just so should God deal with the wicked. It makes perfect sense, though it loses the pots and the heat of the furious burning.

My own attempt –

> Let them be vexed as hot as pots on kindling
> let them be taken as sudden as straw in a whirlwind

– aims to preserve the best of the detail, makes the separate images consistent, and fits the emotional and rhetorical thrust of the poem, as well as the concrete vigour of the similitudes themselves, and their connotations (God the consuming fire, God the whirlwind). In doing this I was working from the spirit of 'that's the kind of thing the poem ought to be saying here, and that's the manner it should be saying it in, vivid, violent, clear.'

The other problem I haven't solved. I think I decided not to. I mean the sudden shifts of person, where in one verse God is addressed directly and the next he's being spoken of in the third person or else speaking himself in the first. I have come to see it as a parallel to what we do in prayer: 'Almighty God, whose Son Jesus Christ fasted forty days in the wilderness, and was tempted as we are etc.' It's as if we are ourselves debating, heart and head perhaps, in the presence of God.

In the same way there's a curious mixture of private soul-searching and open declamation, the former lyrical and confessional, the latter public and liturgical. It's a difficult balance to find a voice for both, especially as they normally sit side by side in the same poem. Sometimes they resolve in a single statement:

> And whatever it was I promised you I would do
> I will do it boldly in public,
> In the very heart of the house of the Lord,
> right in the heart of Jerusalem.

That is the intimate voice, I feel, and it's the one I have opted for in the main: the other one is David Frost's option:

> I will pay my vows · to the Lord:
> in the presence · of all his people,
> in the courts of the house · of the Lord
> even in your midst O Jerusalem.

The psalms remain, in whatever version, an intercommunion between man and God, the micromystery of the individual soul and the macromystery of the great creation. But whatever the conflict within the soul the outcome is always praise. And this must be what is characteristic of the psalms, the way they present praise as a wholesome attitude for all circumstances. And since this is the vital function of the poem, to bring into focus what is good, the suggestion is that these psalms are perhaps as near as we can get to absolute poetry

Earlier versions of these versions have appeared in *Dictes & Measures* (114), *See Me Through* (119), *The Spen River Anthology* (50), and *The Asgill Psalter* (1–20, and the two versions of 150).

Psalm 1

Oh how well off he will be
    whose nose has not been led by know-alls,
    whose feet have not been swept along with the crowd,
    who has not joined in the laughter of those
                    who belittle whatever is decent.
His pleasure is more on the mind of God;
    it is fixed on him in all seasons.
He is sound as a tree that grows beside running water,
    whose autumn will be full of fruit;
His leaves will never lack green;
    his labours will all pay off.
The ones that abandon God will not be so lucky;
    the wind will carry them off like chaff;
In a just society they will have no place;
    on Judgement Day they will not have a leg to stand on.
The ones that seek the Lord, the Lord is already with them;
    but those that get their own way will live to regret it.

Psalm 2

Why are the nations up in arms, and men drawn into insane
    dreams?
The world's rulers are in accord – against God, and the Lord's
    Anointed:
'Old God's authority is at an end – long live the Revolution!'
The Lord in heaven is laughing; to him their threats are a joke.
But one day his top will blow, and his fury flow like lava.
Here on my holy mountain, behold the man, the Anointed –
I say what I heard the Lord speak –
                    You are my Son; this day I have
    begotten you;
The nations are yours for the asking, the ends of the earth your
    estate;
With a sceptre of iron judge them; smash them to smithereens.
Learn wisdom smartly, O Captains, and Rulers, remember your
    place;

Bow to the Lord in fear, and rejoice in him with trembling;
Kiss the Son, stay his displeasure; and beware his infolded fire;
Once it erupts it will engulf
                                    all but the blessed he shelters.

Psalm 3

Lord, see how they multiply, my enemies, against me; hear how
        they taunt
    Even his God deserts him.
Lord, so they say, but I say this: You are still my protector and
        hope,
    you are still the breath of my courage.
Lord, I prayed with my voice; on your faraway hill you heard me:
        so in trust I lay down to sleep, and this morning I rise up in
        faith.
Lord, thousands are after my life, ten thousand; I do not fear
        them.
Lord, you are my help; your unseen hand will chide their
        cheekbones,
    will break their chattering teeth.
Lord, deliverance comes by your hand,
    the hand that blesses your people.

Psalm 4

Disposer of Justice, hear my petition;
        you have saved me in the past from my troubles;
        hear me again, and have mercy.
Men of straw, the honour you do me is dishonour,
        as long as you long for nothing but trash and lies.
Hear this: the Lord knows his own;
        when I call on him he will hear me.
Tremble; be ashamed of your cunning;

14

be honest with yourself; sit in silence;
Do right for itself, not appearance;
   and above all, take God seriously.
Many are asking *When will things get better?*
   Lord, let your face shine down on us.
Just touch my heart, O Lord, and my joy is full,
   richer than harvests of corn and wine
   that break all previous records.
I can lie down in content, and sleep;
   with you alone my comfort, my confidence.

Psalm 5

Hear me, O Lord, and appraise the words of my heart;
   hear what I plead, my Judge, my King, my God.
Doesn't my prayer come up with the morning?
   am I not first in the queue to call on you?
You are not a God to take the part of the villain
   or to enjoy the company of the vile;
The self-important have no importance with you
   and those that hate justice you must hate them as well;
The ones that impose on truth you will expose;
   the ones that sell justice and blood you will hold to account.

But I shall come with confidence into your house
   and bow myself with respect before your presence.
Lord of all justice, give me your guidance now;
   advise me how to answer my enemies.
I put no trust in anything they tell me;
   under their smiles their claws are out to get me;
Their tongues are honey-sweet
   and yet their throats stink like an open grave.
Turn the tables, Lord;
   let them fall in the pit that they have dug;
For their rebellions dispose of them
   for it is you they rebel against in the long run.
And let the ones rejoice who put their trust in you,
   let the battlecry of your name be a hymn of joy;

15

Let them speak your name with pride and with thanksgiving,
    the glorious name that has proved strong to save:
For, Lord, you shall give your blessing to the just;
    the forearm of your favour is his shield.

Psalm 6

O LORD, tick me off, but not in anger,
    take me to task, but not while you are wild.
Make allowances, Lord, I am at the end of my strength;
    I am shaken to the bones, Lord; nurse me back to health.
I am in distress, to the very soul I am;
    O Lord, how long will it last?
Change your mind, Lord; let me off the hook;
    think of your reputation, all Merciful One.
The dead do not remember you at matins;
    in hell they do not sing you the psalm of the day.
I have groaned till I am sick of it,
    I have wet my pillow with tears, the blankets as well.
My eyes are red with weeping, sorrow has made them lined,
    look how my trials have aged me.

Stand back, you that wish me harm, give ground;
    my tears have touched the skirts of the Almighty;
My cry has come to his ears, my heaviness has reached his heart.
They that laughed me to scorn, see shame come upon them,
        suddenly;
    run as they will, their shame keeps pace with them.

Psalm 7

O, LORD MY GOD, my champion I trust in,
    save me from those that are on my tracks
    before like lions they tear my throat out,

tear me in pieces that no one can put together.
O Lord my God, if I have done what I should not,
    if my hands are tarred with guilt,
    if I have let down any that trusted me,
    me who let my enemies off
        who sought me without good reason,
    then may they hunt me, may they corner me,
    may they drag me down to earth and savage me,
    may my pride discolour the dust
        and my honour stain the dirt.
O Lord, arise, let my enemies' rage enrage you;
    rise up for Justice, you who ordained
        that justice must be done;
    let all the people gather around your throne
    when you rise up to sit in judgement on them.
O Lord, who are the judge of all the nations,
    judge me, O Lord, according to my case;
    write down my innocence for all to see;
    the crimes of the unjust, put a stop to them
    and vindicate the ones who have suffered for justice;
    for you alone see to the pith of intentions,
    testing the blood and the guile of the innermost heart.
My shield is the Name of God.
    the champion of every honest heart;
    justly he judges, injustice angers him daily;
    the sword of his justice screams on the whetstone
    against the unrepentant; his bow is ready strung
    and bent, his arrows tipped with sulphur:
    his quarry, blind to justice and to God,
    is busy about his evil, breeding lies;
    he digs a grave for others, digs it deep,
    but it shall be his own;
    the wickedness he cunningly has plotted
    will sever his own head.
O Lord Most High, I thank you for your Justice;
I shall praise your Wonderful Name in song after song.

Psalm 8

O LORD OUR GOD, over ALL THE EARTH
   how FULL OF GLORY is YOUR NAME
     you have written it in stars across the heavens;
     to the shame and silence of your enemies
     it speaks in the mouths of sucklings and of babies
     leaving the wisdom of this world confounded;
     under the mighty vast of heaven's vault
     tricked out with the delicate stars your fingers set there
     what is mere man that you respect him so,
     the kin of Adam that you care about him?
     you created him just two inches short of a god,
     gave him a glorious crown and did him honour;
     you put a sceptre of power into his hands
     and all his fellow creatures under his feet;
     all sheep and livestock, all the feral beasts,
     fowls of the air and fishes of the flood,
     all that wander the pathways of the waters.
O LORD OUR GOD, over ALL THE EARTH
   how FULL OF GLORY is YOUR NAME

Psalm 9

I thank you, Lord, with all my heart I thank you;
I'll repeat the theme again of the wonders that you've done;
I shall enlarge my gladness into exultation,
I shall decorate your name with songs that will praise you.
My enemies stop in their tracks, see them panic and fall;
It is your presence alone that has consumed them.
You heard my case, you gave it consideration,
You the just judge, you have upheld my claim,
The very judge that has judged the mightiest empires
And made them only a name in history,
Their once great cities not even now on the map;
Men look for them today with shovel and spade.
The throne of the Skygod Judge is in the heavens;
Man may not topple it, time will not take its toll;

That seat sits on the world, on every one of us,
And our security is in his verdict;
The honest and the cheated he will insure.
The ones that know your name know they can trust you;
Not one of them can say you have let them down.
So, sing great hymns to God, let his home be Sion,
Remind mankind of all that his hands have done;
Hands that are bloody from judging the oppressor,
Hands that have answered cries of the oppressed.
And Lord, have mercy in my present trouble;
You helped me in days gone by, you were my champion;
Let me have cause to praise you as I did then;
Give me occasion to compose afresh
                              more and more psalms of deliverance.
Your challengers lie in the pits they dug for others;
They spread their nets and got themselves entangled;
That is when you appear, with proverbs of justice,
Of fools that are hoisted with their own petards;
They jump, like lemmings, down to a godless place,
All who preferred a world that was free of God.
And the time will come when the poor will be represented,
When honesty and patience will be rewarded.
Let it come, Lord; and quash the proud man's boast,
Break his lying teeth with the truth and let all men hear it;
Let the fear of God appal them, let them know
That for all their talk they are only ashes and dust.

Psalm 10

Lord, why do you keep your distance?
        In such a crisis as this, why aren't you here?
The proud live off the poor without any check
        and what can a poor man do to protect himself?
The proud gives rein to his schemes,
        his avarice knows no bounds;
He isn't curbed by the thought of God,
        in his eyes God's a fable;
He follows his wayward will, a law to himself,

and can't be criticised;
He tells himself *It pays to be ruthless,*
    nothing will stand in my way.
His mouth tells lies with ease,
    his tongue is a vent of venom, of violence;
His agents penetrate the villages;
    nothing is sacred to him, no innocent safe;
He takes his tax of all, no matter how needy;
    his net is all-embracing, as is his pocket.
He takes his toll, but still he is never content,
    not till there's nothing left for him to take.
He justifies himself: *If God exists*
    He must be much like me;
His right hand will not see
    what the left is doing.

Lord, surely it's time to act;
    but for your hand the poor are completely helpless.
Why can the wicked say, Lord, that you don't care?
    how do they get away with it?
But you who can see all things must see this;
    your scales must measure suffering and wrong;
The distressed count on you,
    you, who are the orphans' father.
Break the arm that is raised against honest men;
    root out corruption, leave it no place to hide.

World without end shall the Lord God reign
    and in his kingdom the nations are all out of fashion:
Lord, you have heard the hurt of the despised,
    in your hands you still hold their hopes
That you shall be their judge and their defender,
    that men made of earth shall reign on earth no longer,
That tinpot gods shall trouble them no more.

Psalm 11

My hideout is the Lord: so why do you advise me
    Take to the hills, fly like a bird away;
    The wicked have you in their sights,
    From their cover they are taking aim
    To deal with the uncorrupted?
When the whole world has gone astray
    where can a good man go?
The Lord is there in his temple,
    his throne high in the heavens;
He looks down on the sons of men,
    in a trice he has summed them up;
He can tell the true from false,
    and the petty bully gets his goat up;
All hell shall be let loose on them
    like a volcano bearing down
    with molten rock and fire on their screaming;
Because God loves justice, and he cannot change,
    and those that love justice he cannot choose but love.

Psalm 12

Comfort me, Lord, because there is no trust left
    between men, no friendship, no fidelity;
Men use their skills to tell lies,
    building up confidence to let their partners down.
The pleasing lips, the tidy tongue,
    God blast them for their blasphemy that said
When we have wrested words to our purpose
    we'll get away with murder.
But this is God's answer: *In defence of the destitute*
    Here I stand, against the persecution of the poor.
I hear their cries, and take them at face value.
The words of God are words indeed, seven times tried in the fire.
Watch over us, Lord, and in threse dreadful days defend us,
In this time when the wicked prosper,
    this time when the very lowest are in control.

21

Psalm 13

How long, O Lord, how long will you forget me? For ever?
How long will you hide your face behind a cloud?
How long shall I be jailed in misery?
How long measure my days in humiliation?
How long do I have to endure the crowing of my abusers?
O Lord my God, it must be long enough:
Bring light to my eyes, before they close in death,
Before my enemies say *At last he's done for*,
Before they declare my trust in you was in vain.
But either way, my hope is in you to the end;
Before my heart fail it shall joy in your mercy and justice;
And I shall sing your praise *now*,
In advance of the love you will show me.

Psalm 14

The clever and conceited have concluded: *There is no God.*
For all their wisdom they are corrupt and vile; what good do
        they do?
From his vantage-point God looked on the sons of Man
        to see if any were looking up to him:
No, not one; they were all concerned with themselves,
        they were every one busy outdoing their neighbours.
They eat my people with unconcern as if they were eating bread;
        what happened to their consciences?
They never call upon their Maker's name
        except to swear, or poke fun at the innocent.
The day will come when fear will overtake them,
        the day when God will show if he exists.
Then he will stand among his chosen people,
        the ones that were despised for choosing him.
Let it come soon, the D-day of deliverance, the doomsday of
        bosses;
        out of Sion he shall judge them all.
The people of Jacob shall all be over the moon
        and Israel shall go raving mad with gladness.

Psalm 15

Lord, who shall you make at home in your private quarters?
    who shall have his house in your hilltop city?
The one that watches his step, and is always right;
    the one that puts the truth above everything;
The one that holds his tongue from slander,
    that tells no tales, that stands by what he says;
The one that has no time for the world's timeservers
    but shows respect to all that respect the Lord;
The one that keeps his word, even when it hurts him;
The one that lends for good and not for profit,
    whose judgement is never swayed by interest.
Such as do all these things need have no fear;
    indeed he is a man after God's own heart.

Psalm 16

I have put my trust in you, Lord, don't let me down;
I told you, Lord, I said *You are my only hope*;
I only delight in those who delight in you.
Those that back other gods are asking for trouble;
You'll not catch me in their cults, at the obscene rituals,
    making my mouth foul with their blasphemous names.
You are my Lord, you are my meat and drink,
    you are my whole inheritance;
The lot whichever you give is a pleasant place
    and my delight is the task you give me to do.
Blessed be God, who is my share of wisdom,
    who gives me counsel even when I'm asleep.
I have granted God the power to guide my steps,
    to stand beside me in every time of trial;
He is my confidence, he is my cheerfulness;
    what have I to fear?
You will not cast my soul to the fires of Sheol
    or to the mouldering mercy of the grave.
You will nurse my trusting steps in the way of life,

you will break my heart with joy at your presence with me:
Pleasures shall fall from your ever-open hand.

Psalm 17

Give ear to my complaint, O Lord, and to my cry your heart;
    Hear my prayer, and see if I speak the truth;
Give judgement as you are minded to,
    Weigh justice in the balance of your eyes.
You have watched my heart, by night as well as day;
    Examined me, and found no evil intent;
My lips have never been led astray
    by the custom of those about me;
Your words have been my constant model;
    They guide my steps, they keep me on firm ground.
I call on you, Lord, because I know you will answer;
    Hear me again, please, hear my urgent prayer;
Show me once more the grace that amazes me,
    Your mighty hand that is sanctuary to us;
Let me be still the apple of your eye;
    Keep me under the shadow of your wings
From the hot breath of those who persecute me,
    Who would destroy me right to the very soul;
Pity is something they have all renounced,
    and this they are proud of;
See how they prowl about me, listen to them roar,
    eager to have me in their hearts' arena,
Lions that raven to the kill,
    young ones that have to prove they have lions' hearts.
Rise up, Lord, show your face, and face them down;
    Come between me and them;
The favour of your arm is worth
    ten shields and twenty swords.
In the height of their pride bring them down to earth;
    they are never content, however much they are loaded:
Sons without number they have, and sons' sons;
    treasure to stock a whole dynasty.
But I shall stand in your presence, if there is justice,

24

and my treasure will be to see you, and to be glad.
My heart you will light up, you will make it shine,
    you will say *Let there be light* in my heart of darkness;
With you beside me I shall put legions to flight,
    I shall effortlessly hurdle a city wall.
The Lord is perfect in everything he does;
    his word is a cert, and a shield to those who want it.
Who but the Lord is God? Who but he is solid?
    it's his strength arms me, he navigates my feet,
He is the spring in my step, my sureness of foot;
    he schools my arms in the arms of war, I can bend a bow
       made of bronze.
Your hand is a shield to me, it shall hold me up;
    it shall lift me up each time I have fallen down,
You clear my path, you put strength into my ankles,
    you give me stamina to stay in long pursuit
So none shall lightly escape your word of justice,
    so they shall not escape my final sword.
You are my battle power;
    you are my plan of attack;
It is you takes the tally of prisoners,
    you who makes me a pavement of their backs.
They will cry out, but who will help them;
    they will even cry out to you, but you will be deaf;
I could grind them to powder, to dust on the wind;
    I could scrape them off my shoes like mud.
You spared me from the horrors of civil war
    and raised me into a lord to preside over nations;
Foreigners, when they hear, shall seek me to rule them.
    strangers I've never heard of, calling me king;
Without a fight they will hand over fortresses,
    pleased to be subjects of one that God defends.
Yes, God is alive, by this the world shall know it,
    by psalms that tell of my deliverance;
God who took my part, who fought beside me,
    God who gave me peoples I never sought.
Yes, Lord, you raise me over my opponents,
    those who raised themselves in vain against me.
I give my thanks to you who are Lord of Nations;
    I give you thanks with songs that exalt your name.
You rescued the king that you yourself anointed;

you have done wonders, you have shown astonishing favour
To David, and to those of David's line.

Psalm 18

Lord, you are my strength; my castle, and the rock it stands on;
    my bodyguard, my shield, my perfect defence;
One call to you, Lord, *deus ex machina*,
    and all my enemies are powerless.
My hands were tied by death behind me, white water dragged me
    away,
    under me opened the chasm of hell, a noose was tight at my
    throat;
But I still had a voice to call upon God, to cry to him out of my
    heart,
    and for all the faintness of my words they still got to him in
    heaven.
Then the earth quaked and heaved, the mountains shook with
    fright,
    his mouth was afire with anger, and wrath made his nostrils
    smoke;
As he moved the sky was ablaze with him, yet pitch-dark under
    his feet;
    his mount was one of the Cherubim, he rode the wings of the
    wind;
With darkness in front of him like a shield and black cloud
    swirling behind,
    hailstones of fire raining down, hot cinders and clouds of
    sulphur;
Then thunder tore the heavens in two, the voice of the Highest
    spoke out,
    words that none could stand against, words of unquenchable
    fire;
On all sides round his arrows were loosed, lightnings flashed from
    his bow;
    the bed that seas had covered heaved into sight,
    the hills were bare to the eye, to their very roots,
    because the Lord had spoken, because your anger was roused.

Then the Lord rescued me, he reached his hand from heaven
      and pulled me out of the swirling waters;
His hand was my deliverer, however many my enemies,
      however well they were armed, however bitter against me;
They had me at their mercy and I was done for,
      but God was my passport to safety, and my safe conduct;
I was his refugee and he was my refuge;
      because I was faithful to him he stood by me;
I honoured him all my life, I kept my hands clean,
      and he rewarded the faith of a simple man;
Yes, those who love you you repay with love,
      those that are loyal find you a loyal Lord;
You are meek and mild to those that are true of heart,
      but the hard-hearted find you are merciless;
You are freedom to the persecuted captive,
      and will make their proud tormentors grovel before them.

Psalm 19

The heavens spell out the glory of God,
      the stars the breadth of his conception;
Day opens up the light of his grace
      and night keeps his purpose secret;
With not one word spoken or language
      or the hearing of any voice
The sounds of the spheres fill the whole of time
      and reach to the limits of space.
He has fixed a special place for the sun
      which bursts from it like a bridegroom
Dressed for his wedding in dazzling splendour,
      or like an athlete on the day of the race
With every atom alert and keen for the off;
      the start is at the dawn of the heavens
And he will not flag till the day itself is finished,
      and everywhere he passes they feel his heat.
What God ordains is perfect,
      the rhythms renew old life;
Whatever he teaches is sound

and the simple who learn it are wise;
The duties he prescribes
    are the cornerstones of pleasure;
The instructions he appoints
    are doors to the understanding;
The awe he inspires is profound,
    and it will never diminish;
The judgements he makes are unerring,
    and show us what justice is;
Gold is not more worth having, heaps of it,
    nor honey more tasty, even the purest honey;
They are guides to us, and warnings,
    and it pays us to live our lives by them.
Who can count all the times we offend unwittingly?
    no doubt I often stink in your nostrils;
Lord, when I do, please cleanse me,
    as many times as I need it;
Clear me of pride and priggishness,
    don't let them master me;
I want to be faultless, Lord,
    I want to be innocent.
May the words that I speak out please you,
    and the thoughts I keep to myself,
O rock-solid Lord,
    my Saviour.

Psalm 20

May God be your answer on the day you need him
    the Name of the God of Jacob your insurance,
May he send assistance from his holy office
    and keep a lookout over you from Sion;
May he remember all your past oblations
    and call to mind your many sacrifices;
May he be pleased to grant you what you ask for
    and to provide what you have so long longed for;
May we put flags out on your day of deliverance

and sing for joy and give to God the glory;
May God grant all your prayer.

Now I declare
    the Lord will have respect to his anointed,
He will reach down his right hand from the height of heaven
    to be his protector, to be his upholder;
Some trust in firepower, some rely on their hardware,
    but we have faith in the Name of the Lord our God;
They go the way of the defeated,
    but we survive, we reap a glorious name.

O Lord, save your anointed,
    and be a powerful answer to our calling.

Psalm 21

The king enjoys your protection, O Lord;
    he is glad of the strength of your power;
You have given him all his heart could wish for,
    you have denied him nothing;
You bless him publicly with prosperity;
    his crown of gold is a halo.
When he begged his life of you, you granted it;
    now day by day he shall reign to the end of time.
His greatest glory is your delivering him,
    that's all his honour and title, his pride and joy.
Still every day you shower more blessings on him,
    though what he prizes most is your own presence.
The king puts all his trust and hope in God;
    that's what he stands on, may the Lord keep him so.
Your enemies will feel the weight of your hand,
    your right hand that will reach out and apprehend them,
A hand that is hot for justice, a hand of fire;
    one touch of it will be enough to consume them.
The world will be rid of them and all their breed,
    and the world will be a better place without them.
They wanted to wrest the sceptre from your hand,

they wanted to rule in your place; it was not to be.
 Their shoulders will be as stepping stones to your feet;
  your bowstring will make music from their faces.
Let us see you, Lord. Let us see how high you are.
  For the highest songs we can make
   will sing in your honour.

Psalm 22

Dear God, my God, why have you abandoned me?
  why are you so far off when I need you so much?
By day, Lord, you are deaf to my entreaties,
  and at night you only answer me with silence.
I know you are there, Lord, I know you are holy as ever,
  worth all the praises Israel can give you.
Our fathers put their trust in you,
  and because of their trust you never let them down;
They looked to you and you respected them,
  you wouldn't let their cries dry on their lips.
But I am looked on with contempt, not seen as a man at all;
  no more than a worm that they tread underfoot.
The lash of their laughter strikes home,
  their amusement is pitiless, it goes on and on;
He trusted in God, they say, and much good it did him;
  look at God's answer, look at what He thinks of him!
But even in my mother's womb you were my hope;
  I hung on you more than my mother's breasts;
You were the inheritance I came into at birth,
  and I called you God as soon as I opened my mouth.
Don't now desert me in the thick of troubles,
  not now when you alone are my only help.
They mass round me like bulls, wild bulls,
  bulls of Bashan pawing the sand;
They pack round me like lions,
  roaring, shaking their manes, stretching their jaws.
My strength is turned to water and leaks away;
  all of my bones seem out of joint;
My nerve is gone to wax,

I can feel it melting inside me;
My tongue is like baked clay,
   it sticks to the roof of my mouth;
I can taste the dust I am made of,
   the dust I am coming to.
My enemies are baying round me,
   they will be in at the death;
Look at the holes they have torn
   in my hands and my feet.
Each bone that I own is in pain,
   though their gloating is harder to bear.
They are sharing my clothes out among them,
   dicing for who gets what.
Lord, don't leave it any longer,
   do it now if you mean to help me,
Save what is left of me from the sword,
   my body the dogs are waiting for;
Come between me and the lions' jaws,
   and the savaging horns of the bulls.

I love your name, I am brother to all who love it;
   together we will praise your name in song.
And praise him with us, if you respect the Lord,
   all of the breed of Jacob, honour him gladly;
All who call Israel father, revere our God:
   who looked down on the oppressed, the poor, the distraught,
And didn't despise them;
   when they besought him, he heard.
In the church of the faithful I will sing from the heart,
   before all that fear you I will keep my word.
Those that hunger for you will be satisfied,
   those that look for you will find you,
And out of their overflowing hearts
   their joy will pronounce your name.
From the ends of the earth they will turn to you,
   in you they will come to themselves;
The races of the world, the divided nations
   will bow together before him,
For he alone is the whole world's King
   and the whole world's praise is his due.
Those that have bowed already to the grave
   shall stand before him, and bow;

Those that have been buried under the clay
 shall rise up clean, and worship;
But I, as I live each moment in his presence,
 shall never die.
My children too will praise him,
 my children and my children's children;
They shall stretch out the glory of his name
 from generation to generation
Of those that are yet unborn,
 in tongues that are yet unheard;
And they shall tell the amazing gospel abroad
 of this great thing that you will accomplish for us.

Psalm 23

I am the Lord's sheep; all that I need I have.
 He pastures me in the greenest meadow,
He waters me at the clearest brooks,
 he sees to it that I thrive.
With care he leads me safely on good paths
 for shepherd's honour;
Even through darkest dales and the threats of death
 I have no fear,
Not with you beside me,
 you with your cudgel and your crook to help me.

You spread me a feast in front of my enemies;
 you shower me with honours, you fill my glass yourself.
All my life long your mercy has dogged my steps,
 and your goodness always bounds ahead of me;
And all my life to come the House of the Lord
 will be my fold, and yours.

Psalm 24

The globe is God's and everything it is full of,
    all of the earth and all that the earth sustains;
He made it like a ball and set it spinning,
    gave it its place among the scheme of stars.

Who dare visit the Lord on his holy mountain?
    who dare walk up to his door?
Him with a clean conscience,
    him with an undissimulating heart,
Him that has never come to terms with lying,
    that has not sacrificed honesty to importance.
To such a man God himself is a blessing,
    just to be owned by him is better than justice.
He that longs for the Lord shall find his fortune,
    and have his inheritance in the God of Jacob.

Stand up, you gates, stand tall,
    swing open wide to let the King come in,
The King whose face is brighter than the sun.
    Who is this King who outshines the sun?
It is the Lord, it is the Almighty,
    who comes victorious from all his battles.
Stand up, you gates, stand tall,
    swing wide as you can to let the King come in,
The King whose face is brighter than the sun.
    Who is this King who outshines the sun?
It is the Lord, it is the Conqueror
    who comes victorious with all his armies.

Psalm 25

Accept the whole heart, O God, I offer you.
Back me up still, Lord; please don't let me go under;
    don't let the so-and-soes get me down.
Choose what they say, you'll stand by those who stand by you;
    not with the loud-mouths, not with the leaky in faith.

Direct my footsteps, Lord, on the right road;
　　be as plain as a signpost;
Each day guide me and teach me;
　　be my rescuer and my hope.
For you I have waited a good long while,
　　and I'll go on till you come.
God, your goodness and mercy
　　go back to the start of my life;
How weak my offences seem
　　in the light of your glorious goodness.
Isn't he amazing; generous; mindful;
　　guiding us sheepheads, giving us protection!
Just so, just right, that's how he is
　　with them that are minded to know him.
Kingly in mercy, have mercy on me,
　　on the angry wound of my sin that seeks forgiveness.
Let any man look to the Lord
　　and he will show him what he needs to know;
Much he will have to give thanks for,
　　and much shall his children inherit.
Now to the saints that need him
　　the Lord shall unbosom his wisdom;
On him my eyes have been fixed,
　　no one else can untie my poor hands.
Please, Lord, please,
　　I am ground down, I am lost;
Quashed and disheartened and tearful,
　　you're the only one I can turn to;
Right from the start my whole life's work
　　was for you, despite all my failings
See how my enemies flourish,
　　look how their hate of me prospers;
Take me away, Lord, please;
　　save me, don't let them destroy me.
Upright and honest preserve me,
　　untouched by corruption, and breakdown;
Waiting for you, Lord, was ... well, hell;
　　but when you turn up ... OI ... Oi ... OI!

Psalm 26

Lord, I appeal to you; haven't I toed the line
    in probity, conscience, and in my trust in you?
Give me what test you will; what I think, what I do,
    put all of it on trial.
I have the measure of your goodness to guide me,
    I have your truth and openness for a yardstick.
I have never haunted the clubs of the empty-headed,
    or put a party-line before simple truth;
The high society of crooks has no appeal for me,
    I have no time for hypocrites and thugs.
Lord, I have always kept my hands clean,
    I have kept in mind the altar I stand before
So my thanksgiving there would be sincere
    and the heart that I lift up have nothing to hide.
Your house, Lord, is for me a place of beauty;
    I am at home wherever you are honoured:
So please, don't lock me up with men of violence,
    with those whose blasphemies come from the heart,
Those with the blood of innocence on their hands
    who hold them out to me in treacherous friendship.
O Lord, have mercy, set me clear of them,
    let everything I do be beyond reproach;
Let me stand upright, my feet on solid rock,
    To praise my Lord, and let everybody hear it.

Psalm 27

God is my sun and my destiny; what should I be afraid of?
    My strength, my protector; what have I got to fear?
The threats of enemies that prowl about me, that try to trip me,
    they are nothing, they are the ones that will stumble.
If a regiment came against me I wouldn't care;
    if a whole army came they wouldn't disturb me.
I have asked just one thing of God, I want nothing more;
    to live with him, every day, in my house or his,
    to enjoy him, and all the beauty he gives rise to.

In his company, under his roof, how can misfortune touch me?
    he will hide me, he will cradle me in his arms;
He will set me up on a pinnacle, with walls about me;
    the enemies way down below are no cause to fear.
But I have cause to praise him, to sing for joy,
    to lavish thanks on him for all he has done.

Hear the prayer, Lord, that my heart addresses;
    hear, and have mercy; let it touch your heart.
You told me always to look you in the eye;
    now I am looking, don't turn away, I beg you;
Even if you are angry, I am still your child,
    I am still your friend, I am still devoted to you.
You have always been my support, don't take it away,
    don't let me down now when I need you most;
My father may let me down, and even my mother,
    but not you, Lord; not you.
Show me how to proceed and what to do;
    don't let the envious get the better of me;
Let us walk together straight through their ambushes,
    let us confound their lies, make them stick in their throats.
But whatever befall, I know this for sure:
    I shall see the goodness of the Lord in the land of the living.
So wait on the Lord;
    be strong, be courageous, be stubborn;
    but wait on the Lord.

Psalm 28

I call on the source of my strength, who is the Lord;
Do not turn a deaf ear to me; I am a dead man, if you do.
Your ear is tuned to mercy, and that's what I ask;
Hear me and help; look at my hands raised towards you.
Don't mix me up with the wicked, don't let me sink with them,
Who court their neighbours with smiles, the better to guile them.
May their deeds be justly rewarded as they deserve;
Let their own hands witness against them what they have done;
May they who belittled the hands of God fall into them.

I bless the name of the Lord who has heard my prayer.
The Lord is my strength and my shield and I trust in him.
In him my heart dances for joy, my soul is in song.
The Lord is the source of our strength, and his strength shall keep
Those his own hand has commissioned.

Lord, be our defender, and bless the ones you have chosen;
Be our good shepherd and we shall be in good hands.

Psalm 29

Give the Lord his due, you who are his sons,
Give him his due, worship and honour and thanks;
Put on your smartest dress, and kneel before him.
The voice of the Lord that stirs the mighty waters,
The voice of the Lord that bellows in thunder,
The voice of the Lord that screams in the teeming rain,
The voice of the Lord is power, and majesty,
The voice of the Lord that breaks the hearts of cedars,
The voice of the Lord that flattens the forests of Lebanon,
Sirion skips like an ox to hear it, Lebanon like a calf,
The voice of the Lord that explodes the mountains of fire,
The voice of the Lord that causes the desert's contractions,
That makes the desert of Kadesh writhe in labour,
The voice of the Lord that speaks in the pains of labour,
That tears the leaf from the tree, the tree from the ground.
To God in his Temple everything gives glory, glory for ever,
Who gives his strength to his people, who gives his people peace.

Psalm 30

I exult in you, Lord, because you have been my support,
    you have not let my enemies have the last laugh;
In my agony, Lord, I called you;

you healed me, you gave me redress;
I lay in the heaps of the dead, but you brought me out,
 my spirit was gone, but you brought me back to life.
Sing glad songs to the Lord, you who are saints of his,
 delight in his holiness, in the beacon of his name.
His anger is past in a minute;
 his love lasts longer than life;
Sorrow may make the night darker,
 but with the next morning comes joy.

In my time of prosperity I had said
 Nothing will bend my spirit;
You had given me such good promises,
 you had given me such strong faith;
But you took your face away from me
 and depression overcame me;
Then, Lord, I called for help to you,
 I prayed on my knees with tears;
Will a nervous breakdown honour you?
 what good will my madness do?
Will dumbness profit or praise you?
 will dull stupour exalt your name?
Hear me, O Lord, and help me;
 remind me of your grace.
And you turned my depression to dancing,
 and lifted the weight off my soul,
So my spirit will never stop singing now
 and the psalms will go on and on;
My Lord, my God,
 my theme to the limit of time.

Psalm 31

In you, O Lord, I have put all my trust;
 honour my faith, as you are dependable and good.
Hear me and come to my rescue,
 be my defending castle, as well as the rock it stands on;
And be my counsellor, and guide,

38

and give me wisdom, for the sake of your good name.
They have caught me in a net they set out for me,
    but you are my helper, I know you can get me out.
All that I am I gladly put in your hands
    and you, the Lord of Truth, you will redeem me.
Fools make false gods for themselves, and of themselves,
    but I put my trust in nothing but you yourself.
I rejoice in your love because it never runs out;
    you saw me in need, and you did something about it.
You did not leave me to my enemies' mercy,
    but freed my spirit to breathe, and my feet to fly.

I call on your goodness again, Lord, in this new trouble;
    the stress of it darkens my eyes, it breaks body and soul.
What strength I had my guilt has eaten away,
    grinding my spirit, and grieving has made me old.
My enemies find it funny, my neighbours look down their noses;
My friends are mortified with embarrassment;
    if we meet in the street they pretend they haven't seen me;
I am put out of mind
    as much as if I had died the year before;
I am like a broken jug,
    thrown away and thought nothing more about.
I have heard their whispering, I have seen their heads together,
    and their threats and plots against me I can guess.
But in you, O Lord, I have put all my trust;
    I call you my God, and my fate is in your hands.
Save me from all the best-laid schemes
    their subtle heads have devised.
Let the sun of your face look down on me,
    and your love that never runs out.
When I pray to you, Lord, let it not be in vain;
    unlike the prayers of those who make light of you,
Who are in hell already
    and soon their lips will be dumb;
Lips that have spent their service
    speaking against the decent, humble and right.
How good your goodness is,
    biding its time of blessing;
But it will be seen by all the eyes of men
    lighting on those who waited in hope for you.
Your presence has been like wings about them

that hunters would have made their prey;
Your mercy has been like a roof above them
     that storms of rage would have destroyed.
And I bless the name of the Lord,
     who saved me when I was like a city besieged,
Who saved me because of his love that never runs out.
In my fear and folly I said
     The Lord has let me down.
But you had heard me when I called for help.
So love the Lord with all your hearts,
     all of you men who call yourselves his saints,
For to those who love the Lord he gives the Lord
     and denies himself to those who forgo his grace.
Be strong, therefore, the Lord will be your courage,
     you who have put the whole of your trust in God.

Psalm 32

How lucky the man whose faults have been forgiven,
     whose foolishness is not remembered against him;
The height of fortune! if God has nothing against him
     his soul is as free as any soul could be.
While I kept my misdemeanours to myself
     I was eaten alive by the guiltiness inside me;
It was no joy to think of you,
     I couldn't even bear to mention your name;
I knew you only as a threat
     and inside of me my spirit was all dried up.
Then I came to my senses, I said *I will tell him all,*
     I'll make a clean breast of it, I won't hold anything back.
And you were delighted to forgive me;
     that's what you're like, and I should have known it.
Let everyone who will, then, pray to you,
     and should the whole world flood again he will safely float.
Distress, anxiety, misfortune,
     how can they touch me while I have you to turn to?
I call to mind the words of many a psalm,
     how they recall so many past deliverances.

I'll give you some good advice,
  I'll give you the most profitable instruction,
A word in your ear for whatever you turn your hand to.
Don't be like a beast, like a horse or a mule,
  who has to be shown the way with a bit and bridle;
That's the way of a fool,
  he asks for the whip.
But the man whose hope is in God has a hand on his shoulder,
  and it strengthens, it directs, it shows him fondness.
So thank your lucky stars you are his;
  let the heart that is wise be over the moon in him.

Psalm 33

Enjoy the Lord, you who love what is good;
  if you are just, it will be your pleasure to praise him.
Tell your thanks on the harp and on the fiddle;
  tell it on the ten-stringed rotta.
Sing something avant garde;
  something not done before, something brilliant;
Something you can sing your heart out in;
  something as true as the word of the Lord is true;
Something enduring like that;
  something he might be proud of.
The Lord loves true art and true justice,
  and his earth is made with a love that never runs out.
One word from him and the heavens came into being,
  and out of his breath the orders of angels filled them.
He held in his hand the seven seas in a bottle,
  and blessed the earth with the treasures of the deep.
The earth and everything in it should fear the Lord,
  all creatures be in awe of his wit and power.
He spoke, and it happened;
  he commanded, and things were made.
He brings to nothing the policies of nations,
  he overturns the peoples' plans and pronouncements;
But the Lord's designs can never be frustrated,
  and his mind shall be known in every generation.

The land whose God is the Lord can count itself lucky,
    its people he has chosen to call his own.
From heaven the Lord looks down on the race of Adam;
    over all the earth there isn't a thing he misses;
He sees whatever we do, but more than that
    he knows the heart from which any action springs.
No army is big enough to defend a king;
    no strength is great enough to preserve a hero;
No horse has strength or stamina enough
    to help his getaway from the weight of God.
But those who fear the Lord have God for a lookout,
    those who count on his love that never runs out,
He will look after them and be
    their food in famine, deliverance in death.
We have waited on the Lord, we have banked on him;
    He alone is our hope and our only help.
We trust in one who will not let us down;
    that's why our hearts have good reason to be glad:
And as much as we trust you, Lord, as much as we hope,
    may the love that never runs out be our reward.

Psalm 34

All my days I will bless the Lord;
    always my lips shall speak good of his kindness.
Being his, I will glory in him;
    let the humble hear and join in praise with me.
Come, all who are minded to honour his name
    and let us share together our hallelujahs.
Duly I prayed to him when I was in need;
    duly he answered and set my mind at rest.
Each one who seeks him eventually will find him;
    he will light up their faces with sudden joy;
For the poor in spirit have a Father in heaven,
    and all his wealth is at their command.
Guardian angels are night and day on hand
    to preserve God-fearing souls in hardship.
He is the man of supreme taste among men

who has for himself tasted the goodness of God.
In fear of the Lord there is prosperity;
    having God, what more can you have?
Just men find in him whatever they need,
    but the others are never satisfied.
Knowledge is good, and the first thing you should know
    is your place, with God above you.
Life and all of its blessings you can have
    if you set store by a few well-tested maxims:
Mind your tongue, so it doesn't lead you astray,
    so it never licks the allurement of a lie;
Never do what you think wrong; always do what you should;
    let peace be precious to you, and help others to it;
Open are the eyes of the Lord to the needs of the honest.
    and open his ears to their prayers;
Pronounced on the workers of wrong is the sentence of God,
    even before they do it their doom is determined;
Ready to help the just, though, before they ask;
    he is impatient to hear their prayers, and help them;
So keenly he shares the tears of the broken-hearted,
    so keen to lift the spirits of the downcast;
Through all the troubles that fall to a good man's lot
    the Lord sustains him and turns them into blessings;
Unbroken his bones and his spirit,
    however much tested and tried;
Vainly the wicked assault him,
    they hate him and kill him in vain;

Yes, the Lord will set free the souls of those who love him,
    and acquit the failings of any who trust in him.

Psalm 35

Campaign, O Lord, against those who campaign against me;
    attack them who have put me under attack;
Take up your shield and help me;
    keep them that hunt me at bay with the point of a spear;
Let me hear your comforting words

I am still your saviour.
May those that were after my blood meet shame and disgrace;
    may those that came out to destroy me return with a
        whimper;
May they fly like chaff in the wind from the angel of God;
    in dark, in mire underfoot, with the angel of God behind
        them.
For no good cause they made me a net to be caught in;
    for no good cause they dug me a pit to fall in;
For the cause of good, may their plans rebound upon them;
    may the net catch them, may they fall in their own pit.
Then I will cheer, then I will bless the Lord;
    my old bones will sing, *Who is like you, O Lord,*
Who saves the poor from those who have power over them,
    and the honest soul from those who would grind him down?
They bring their trumped-up charges against me;
    they wear me out with pointless interrogation.
In the past I did them good but they take no heed of it,
    so eager are they to have me done away with;
And yet when they were in need, I prayed in sackcloth,
    I fasted for them, I disfigured myself;
Had it been my dying brother I couldn't do more,
    no, I couldn't give my mother more heartfelt grief;
But come misfortune, they are in league with her;
    they join the crowd that kicks a man that is down;
They never tire of jeering, no, on and on,
    nothing will stop them short of my destruction.
How long can you take it, Lord?
    how long can you witness such unwarranted hatred?
How long must I listen to their roaring,
    and bear the sight of their claws and teeth,
Before you snatch me away from their gloating eyes,
    before I compose a psalm of thanksgiving for you?
Those who deride me deride my God as well;
    see to it, Lord, they don't have the last word;
Their mouths have lost all use of decency;
    profanity of the tongue now governs the heart;
Their mouths are full of violence and lies
    and satisfaction at my helplessness.
Lord, you have seen it all, what have you to say?
    Don't leave me to their mercy.
Rise up, let justice win the day,

and put my case for me, my Lord and God.
You are the one to judge me, you and no other;
    these gloating judges have no time for truth;
Don't let their hideous triumphing go unchallenged,
    who swear the last word has been said, and that against me.
May all who enjoy my disgrace and revel in it
    come to swallow their words;
May they be covered in shame and embarrassment
    who loaded shame and mockery on me.
But may the ones who looked to see me vindicated
    give glory to the Lord,
Who is his servant's pride and prosperity.
    And I shall never tire of giving praise
To you who are just, to you that all just men turn to.

Psalm 36

Sin speaks to the inmost heart of the man without principle;
    he has no fear of God and is proud of it;
In his own eyes he is highly intelligent;
    if he is found out, he reckons, he'll get away with it.
He has learnt to be convinced by his own lies;
    he has lost all contact with judgement, all sense of good.
Even his dreams are dark with machinations;
    nothing is too evil for him to contemplate.
But your love that never runs out, Lord, reaches to heaven;
    your goodness is more expansive than the sky;
Your judgement is sound and strong as the Himalayas;
    your wisdom deeper than the deepest sea.
O God, whose care extends to man and beast,
    how wonderful is your love that never runs out!
Under the shade of your mighty motherly wings
    all creatures of the good earth find sanctuary;
The house of plenty you made shall supply their needs;
    they shall drink of the pleasures you created for them.
All life looks back to you as its source;
    all light goes back to your brightness.
May those who are yours have love that never runs out;

may honest men rejoice in the God of the just.
But preserve me from the fate of the proudfoot tyrant,
    and the reward of red-handed violent men;
They grovel about where they fell, gritting their teeth;
    their legs are as broken clay, they are down forever.

Psalm 37

Are you incensed because the wicked do so well?
    Do you envy them their success? Forget it.
    They may flourish like leaves, but remember autumn is
      coming.
Be wise; do good, and trust the Lord;
    Mind your own business, leave others to theirs;
    Set your heart on God, he will look after you.
Confide in the Lord, commit all your dealings to him;
    With him as your backer how can you fail to prosper?
    The good of your name will shine like the sun in the sky.
Don't be upset by others that prosper dishonestly;
    They get their way, yes, but at what a cost;
    Don't worry; God's mercy is more than money.
Envy will do you no good, neither will anger;
    You know the dishonest will get their just deserts;
    But those who rely on God have a fortune in him.
For a little time the wicked may rule the roost;
    A little time, and no more; others supplant them;
    But in the end the land will revert to the humble.
Green with envy, the wicked detest the honest;
    They feel derided; God derides them indeed;
    He knows the ending of their curious plans.
Hatred of weakness, of good, excites them to action;
    They are armed with sword and bow and pocket-book;
    Weapons they lived by but yet will be their undoing.
Innocents have a power unknown to the wicked;
    The power of arms, of armies, of allies will fail;
    Yet the Lord, unseen, will preserve his own forever.
Justice demands that the Lord will provide for the just;
    Misfortune, oppression, will never distress them long;

They will come, with him, through famine, and war, and
    flood.
Kings of the castle may think themselves secure
    But they will fall as sure as autumn leaves;
    They will burn as rubbish, and even their smoke will vanish.
Loans to the wicked rarely get paid back,
    But the Lord will repay the good and the bad in his time;
    The good are generous givers, and so is our God.
Men with a mind to be upright sons shall be so;
    The Lord will hold them steady on their feet;
    From time to time they may stumble, but won't fall down.
Never have I seen a good man begging his bread,
    Not from when I was young to my old age now;
    He always has something to spare, for friends, for the needy.
Order your days; do good; make peace where you can;
    God who loves justice will always favour the just;
    His law will deal with the lawless and their kind.
Possession of lands will pass to those who deserve them;
    Peace follows justice; with peace comes prosperity;
    Who will remember the names of past grasping landlords?
Reason and rhyme will season a good man's language:
    A level head is matched with a witty heart;
    Workman's words that hit the nail on the head.
Stealth is the wicked man's trade, and seeming important;
    Getting the weak in their clutches is their profession;
    But the Lord will not let them keep the fruits of their labour.
Trust in the Lord; he will keep you out of their hands;
    You will yet live to see the land you love rejoicing;
    You will see those that ruined it come down themselves to
    ruin.
Up to all sorts of tricks, the unworthy will rise;
    I have seen them dining in their successful villas;
    I have passed again, and seen them gone and forgotten.
Virtue and honesty leave good things behind them
    Worthy to carry on a good man's name;
    But they try to conceal their names, the disgraced one's
    children.
When trouble comes to the good, the Lord is their lawyer;
    He will take their case, he will use the law to save them;
    Because they were innocent; because they trusted in him.

Psalm 38

O Lord, correct me, but please, not while you are angry;
    chastise me as you will, but not while you're seeing red.
Your arrows have hit their mark,
    your hand has bruised me all over;
The marks of your fury cover the whole of my body;
    I know I have sinned; my body is paying for it;
My head is bowed down with shame,
    and my body with punishment;
I was a fool, but now sickness makes me disgusting;
    bent double with pain, flat on my back with exhaustion;
I walk about like one who is deep in mourning;
    I am racked with fire, a fever has taken me over;
I am numb, I am all over bruised,
    I start a new groan before I have finished the last one;
O Lord, you hear them, I haven't tried to hide them;
    I haven't made a secret of my distress;
My pulse is up, I have no strength left,
    my eyes are dull and unseeing;
My friends keep away from me,
    even my relatives have stopped their visits.
But those who wish me dead are full of themselves,
    plotting and slandering and tittle-tattling;
I act as if I am deaf, I will not hear them;
    I won't defend myself to them, I play dumb.
I put my hope in you, Lord;
    if they're to be answered, you're the one that will do it.
I said, *Don't let them crow over me,*
    don't let them have the last word in a gloating obituary.
I slip like others, I'm not the man to hide it;
    I make no excuses, I'm sorry, I kiss the rod;
But many will see their own malign success
    in my humiliation, many that hate me, men I've never
        harmed;
Many who are inclined to side with evil
    with no good cause except a dislike of good.
But you won't fail me, Lord, you won't let me down,
    not when I put my trust in you such as I do.

Psalm 39

I made a resolution to hold my tongue;
    I would keep my mouth shut rather than speak amiss;
While reporters were in earshot I clamped my teeth,
    I couldn't have said much less if I had been dumb;
But the more restrained I was the more I seethed;
    and now I have to speak out before I explode.
Lord, remind me of my funeral, that my days are numbered;
    remind me each day I am walking on a tightrope;
My years are but minutes to you, my whole life nothing;
    man for all his pride is a puff of wind, a potential ghost;
With trouble and toil he converts his days into wealth
    that he can't take with him, or say what good it will do:
And where have I set my hope, Lord?
    Only on you.
Save me from all my follies and things ill-done
    that fools have every reason to condemn;
I shall be quiet, I have no right to complain,
    because I only endure what you ordain me;
But please, Lord, no more;
    the blows, one after another, have worn me out;
When you take up the punishment of a man's wrong
    it takes away whatever is dear to him;
    the life that's left is but a walking shadow.
Lord, have a heart and hear my prayer;
    let my crying like a child upset your nerves;
I'm a poor traveller you are bound to shelter
    with little time to stay, like all my fathers;
Please, soften your anger; please, speak to me kindly again
    before my days are done, before it's too late.

Psalm 40

I waited on the Lord, Oh how I waited!
    at last he heard me, he gave me his attention.
Out of the pit he lifted me, out of the mud and mire;
    he set my foot on rock, and I stood upright.

He taught me a new song, gave me a new kind of singing,
    a new way of praising God.
Many will be overawed when they come to hear it;
    they will come to want the Lord our God for themselves.
How lucky is he who dares to trust in God,
    who escapes from the trust of unsound men
    and from unsound institutions!
O my Lord God, what things you have managed!
    How good you have been to us! What more could you do?
I could easily make a start to count my blessings
    but could I ever get to the end?
It wasn't sacrifice that pleased you;
    it wasn't anything offered like payment;
It was rather an ear that wanted to hear you,
    a real desire to hear your actual voice.
What use are sacrifices or any amount of offerings
    unless they go to please you?
Yes, they are offered according to the law,
    the text is observed in each particular;
But, Lord, I want to please you for myself,
    I want the law in my heart, not just on the page.
I advertise your goodness far and wide,
    in general assembly and private conversation.
You know this, Lord;
    I have never kept your miracles to myself;
I have made speeches and psalms about your mercies,
    about your providence, about your comforting words.
So now, Lord, be true to what I have said about you;
    bear out my trust in your love that never runs out;
Now when the cards are stacked against me,
    when all my follies have come home to roost;
Thick and fast they come, they are overwhelming;
    there's more of them than I've got hair on my head.
Come quickly, Lord, to my help
    and save me from them.
Those that think to destroy me shall come to shame;
Those that would see me hurt shall see themselves hurt;
Those that would crow at my fall shall cry at my fame:
But those that would please the Lord shall learn
    the only way to please God is to enjoy him;
Those that would praise the Lord shall know
    the only way to praise God is to enjoy him.

So, though I am abandoned and in need
    the Lord is ever with me;
Sure as day comes, you will come in good time to my rescue;
    but don't leave it too long, Lord. Not too long.

Psalm 41

How well-off is the man who looks after the poor;
    the Lord will do the same for him when need arises;
The Lord will preserve him, the Lord will prosper him,
    the Lord will protect him from his enemies' spite;
The Lord will nurse him on his sick-bed,
    the Lord will bring him back to health and strength.

Lord, have mercy on me, that is my prayer,
    restore my blemished soul that has sinned against you.
My enemies are gloating over me;
    He won't last long, they say; his line is finished;
My visitors all come with empty greetings,
    eager for bad news, keen to pass it on;
My enemies have put their heads together,
    whispering, smiling, waiting for the worst;
He is under a curse, they say,
    confined to his bed, he will never leave it again;
And even the friend I trusted, who ate at my table,
    consents to put the boot in now I am down.
But you can restore me, Lord, you can raise me up,
    and that will show them;
By that I shall know you delight in me, you forgive me;
    so take the untimely triumph out of their mouths;
And raise me, Lord, and be my health and strength,
    and keep me always under your careful eye;
And blessed be the good Lord, God of Israel,
    as long as time shall last. Amen. Amen.

Psalm 42

As the hunted deer longs for water
    that's how I long for you;
My whole soul thirsts; for you, for the living God;
    when will it be, when I come into your presence?
Morning and night I have my fill of tears;
    Where is your God? they say; every day without fail.
My heart is downcast, yet I cling to the time
    when together we processed to the Temple of God,
How we marched, how we sang,
    how our souls were in their element!
Soul, now what depresses you?
    why the tragedy queen?
Do you think God isn't coming?
    Do you think he's tired of your thanking him?
No, I will thank him before I need to,
    I'll give him all the encouragement I can;
The more I'm down, the more I'll cry up his love;
    even if Jordan flood, and the waters off Hermon,
And those off Mizar came cascading down,
    the seas as well came flooding in
Wave after wave, and each one overwhelming me.
But the Lord will come with the dawn,
    with love that never runs out;
Morning and night I shall praise his name
    and the whole of my life be a prayer.
That's why I sing out even now
    Lord, my impregnable fortress,
You haven't forgotten me, have you?
    You haven't given my enemies their way
Because you like me in sackcloth?
    Where is your God? they say,
Every day without fail.
    Soul, now what depresses you?
Why the tragedy queen?
    Do you think the Lord isn't coming?
Do you think he's tired of hearing thanks?
    No, I will thank him before I need to;
I will give him all the encouragement I can.

Psalm 43

Speak for me, Lord, and be my Judge as well,
     against that class that will neither reason nor pray;
Plead my case, uphold my cause
     against the licensed liar and the man of malice.
Since you are my only defence, O God,
     why aren't you here to defend me?
You like the look of me in mourning?
     Is being made a fool of good for the soul?
One word from you, Lord,
     just an appearance, just for one moment,
And all will be put to rights;
     I shall be sitting in heaven
Gazing on goodness, smiles all round,
     eyes full of the tears of gladness,
Playing my harp with the others,
     joining in all the choruses.
My soul, what's wrong with you?
     Why have you got the hump?
I tell you, he's coming.
     Why don't you practise Thanksgiving?
Why not make up a Victory Hymn?

Psalm 44

Our fathers have told us the tale, O Lord,
     and our ears were eager to hear it
Of amazing deeds you did in their days
     and your works in the world before them;
You drove the occupiers from the land to plant your people in it;
You dispossessed the settled peoples to give your folk a home;
The land was won for our fathers not by their swords,
     not by their strength or courage such as it was,
But by your arm alone, by your right hand,
     by your face that shone like the sun and favoured us.
You are my God and King, you are the strength of Jacob;
     your name is enough to disperse our enemies.

53

I do not trust in my bow, or my sword to save me;
  only in you who will put them all to flight.
Our pride is in our God;
  him we will praise as long as suns rise and set.
But today, Lord, why today do you humble us,
  why are we fighting on our own without you?
We turn our backs, we run in all directions;
  foreigners fill their knapsacks with our treasures;
You have left us to the kind mercy of the butcher;
  we must hide in foreign countries as we can;
You have sold your people and got nothing for us,
  just thrown us away;
You have made us the laughing-stock of neighbour nations;
  they spit on us and laugh;
You have made our name a joke, a word of contempt;
  even the lowest now look down on us;
Look where I will disgrace is always in front of me,
  I am ashamed even to own my name;
It's become a word of abuse on foreigners' lips
  and dogs me viciously wherever I go.
Though all this has come to pass, you are still our God;
  we still stand by our faith in you;
We have not looked to some other protector;
  we have not turned our hearts elsewhere;
Even when monsters of hell have turned their spite on us;
  when dragon-smoke covered our heads and filled our lungs.
If we had set aside the name of our God,
  if we had prayed and sacrificed to some other,
You would know about it, you would have seen it,
  you who see even the secrets of the heart.
But it's with your name in our hearts we are done to death;
  we are your sheep, slaughtered and offered to foreign gods.
So wake up, Lord. What's keeping you?
  Get up, don't let us down till it's all too late.
Why so shy? Do our sufferings embarrass you?
  We are down as low as we can be. We are in the pits.
Get up, while there's still just time to save us;
  save us, if only for your own self's sake.

Psalm 45

My heart is on fire to write this psalm
    and its subject is the honour of the King;
My tongue is so eager to tell it
    it will need the sharpest of secretaries to take it down.

Your beauty is more than mortal,
    grace speaks on your lips,
The blessings you have from God
    will never be taken from you.
You put on glory with your armour,
    you put on judgement with your sword;
When you ride out
    justice and truth go with you.
Your right hand will leave terrible things behind it;
    under your hail of arrows nations will fall;
The enemies of the King will fall,
    their very hearts will fail them.
Your throne is a throne of God, it will last forever;
    the sceptre in your right hand is justice itself.
You have been the friend of right, the scourge of wrong,
    so God himself makes you his anointed one;
Your glory and honour are greater than all your fellows',
    your gladness greater than theirs.
Your garments breathe the scents of myrrh and cassia;
    out of your palace of ivory music greets you.
Your court is filled with the noblest daughters of kings;
    your queen at your right hand shall be resplendent,
        honoured and dressed in the finest gold of Ophir.

Listen, my daughter, hear what I have to tell you:
    forget where you came from, forget your father's house;
Your person and beauty are for your Lord's delight,
    so do for the King whatever he asks of you;
You shall be honoured of all;
    the noblest in the land shall look for your favour.

She enters the palace in glory, in cloth-of-gold,
    yet nobler than all her show is the soul of her.
Broidered in gold her maids of honour bring her,
    bridesmaids, into the presence of the King;

Music, gladness and dance escort them
    into the palace, unto the throne of joy.
Your fathers will give way and leave your heart
    to fill with sons worthy to follow them,
To rule and reign and make their peoples proud.

I shall declaim the honour of your name
    from now till the generations are no more,
Till voices cease,
    till all the nations praise you.

Psalm 46

God is our refuge, God is our relief,
    an ever-ready help in trouble;
When the earth quakes we shall not be afraid;
    when mountains slide into the sea,
When tidal waves sweep over the land,
    when mountains shake with fire and thunderclaps.
God is our refuge,
    and his city is graced with healing streams;
He lives there himself,
    it will never be overthrown;
He comes with the break of day
    to protect and provide for it.
Nations shall come to blows,
    powers will rise and fall,
The earth itself will crumble and cower
    when his voice speaks.
But the Lord of Legions fights with us,
    the God of Jacob is our castle wall.
Come and inspect the plans and works of the Lord;
    look at the ruins he has engineered.
Over every foot of earth he has stamped out war,
    he has made all armaments redundant;
The bow is broken, the spear is snapped in two,
    the submarine is gone to scrap.

Shush! I am God, you know.
The nations are under my thumb,
everything on earth is.

The Lord of Legions fights with us,
the God of Jacob is our castle wall.

Psalm 47

Clap till your hands are ringing, all you people,
cheer the name of God till you have no voice.
The Lord is so high above us that we are nothing;
he made the earth and can do what he pleases with it.
Nations shall bow before us at his bidding;
people we never knew are prostrate at our feet.
He chose out himself the land he apportions us;
the land he gave to Jacob out of his love.
God climbs to his throne and the cheering is deafening;
the trumpet fanfare can only just be heard.
Join in, sing praises, don't be left out,
join in the glory that we give him.
God is King over all the earth;
magnify him for all you are worth;
He is King over every nation;
he is Lord of our salvation;
The lords of the Gentiles are at one
with the lords of the sons of Abraham;
All the lords of the earth are the children of God,
and he is their Father over them.

Psalm 48

God is great and well worth the glory we give him,
    in the city where he's at home, his holy mountain Sion;
City of cities, the whole world's pride and pattern,
    the pole of all man's hopes;
For the Lord is King there,
    he himself is its splendour, its defence.
Let kings and armies come against her,
    let them make common cause to take her,
Yet they will be abashed where she looks down,
    panic will strike them, fear will put them to flight;
Like women in the contractions of labour
    look at them trembling;
Like Phoenician galleys when the east wind drives them
    look at them terrified, look at them all at sea.
It's not just hearsay, we witnessed it ourselves,
    the city of God, the city of the Lord of Legions,
The city God has established
    to honour his name from now to the end of time.
Within the Temple of God
    we offer in ritual the story of your love;
We give your name the glory we think it's worth
    and send our psalms to the very ends of the earth.
In your right hand is the gift of justice;
    the hill of Sion is proud to house your court;
The daughter-cities of Judah share her pride,
    happy to prosper under your wise jurisdiction.
So beat the bounds of Sion in slow procession,
    count all her fortress towers,
Size up the walls,
    study the architecture of her palaces
Till you can pass the scale and details on
    to generations that are yet unborn.
God is like that,
    God who will stand for ever,
God who will be our wisdom and our salvation.

Psalm 49

Now hear this, it concerns you;
    this is a lesson for all to hear,
        rich man, poor man, beggarman, thief;
Let the wise value wisdom,
    let the discerning take my words to heart,
        let them weigh the truth of prophecy.
Why should I worry in times when evil prospers,
    when I am hounded and despised,
        when those who have made it wallow in their power?
Can a man worm his way into God's favour?
    Can he plead the importance of his place?
        Can he buy off his destiny with his wealth?
He can't. He could never afford it.
    And if he could he'd be shelling out for ever,
        he would never consent to face the fact of death.
Even the wisest die, that's true,
    but the stupid, do they come off any better?
        Do they keep their gains? Are their graves more
        comfortable?
Yet they carry on as if there is no tomorrow,
    as if their businesses will keep them in business,
        as if their names on labels and lands
        will keep them from being 'late'.
But man is no better than livestock in the main:
one day, as is usual, he is fed and watered;
    the next day, like it or not, he's led
        and slaughtered.
That's the lot of the man who doesn't think,
    of him and all his hangers-on;
        and those who walk in his shoes will find the same.
Like sheep they are herded into hell
    by Death who is their shepherd
        and the dogs that gladly and loudly do his bidding.
No one remembers them on earth
    and under it their bodies stink and rot;
        where just men rule, their souls are only shadows.
My life, though, is in the hands of God;
    death has no power over it, nor hell,
        except by his allowance.
So never envy a man his wealth or power,

his person, his importance, his prestige;
    he must leave every scrap of it behind.
He must leave all his flatterers and friends,
    his power to purchase what he would, or who,
        his precious chattels other people fancied,
And go where all the wealthy went before,
    all his important, titled predecessors,
        into a place where no one knows his name.
For man is no better than livestock in the main:
    one day, as is usual, he is fed and watered,
        the next day, like it or not, he's led
        and slaughtered.

Psalm 50

The Lord God, the only God, has sent word
    and the whole world has to come to his summons
        from the sun's first rising to when it sets for good.
Here comes the shekinah, out of regal Sion;
    he comes with a purpose, his mouth is about to open.
He is dressed in a robe of fire;
    it wreathes and it rages about him;
        it burns everything in his path.
He orders the heavens above and the lowly earth,
    he orders everything that he has made
        to witness the judging of his people.
Gather the ones who are mine,
    who bound themselves to me,
        who sealed themselves to me with sacrifices.
It is God himself who sits in the judgement seat
    and all the heavens look on to see justice done.

Listen to me, my dear ones,
    I have this to say against you.
        I am God, the one who made you.
It isn't your churchgoing I find fault with,
    your prayers and offerings regular as clockwork.
I don't exactly need your sacrifices

or your animals: I'm not a pauper.
You'll find my brand on every one of your cattle,
my mark on every sheep on a thousand hills;
I don't need rings to tell me which pigeon is which,
I own the wild rabbits that nobody else lays claim to.
If I am hungry I don't have to turn to you,
I own the whole supermarket of the world.
Do you think your overdone steak is my delight?
Do you think my favourite tipple is billy-goats' blood?
No, give me your private selves,
your most inward selves,
and whatever you give your word on, see you do it.
Turn to me frankly in your need and I'll help you;
The time to give me thanks is when you mean it.

God's message to his enemies is this:

What right have you to open your mouths
against the very one
who gave you mouths to open?
You who won't be told,
no, not even for your own good;
who turn your backs on me while I'm speaking to you.
You find out a man's a thief, you ask for a lesson;
your neighbour commits adultery, you say 'So what?'
Your mouths are full of smut and swearing;
if slander come your way you're eager to spread it.
No one is in your good books, not even your brother;
not even your mother's son escapes your smearing.
All of these things you've done, and because I was silent
you reckoned I was like you at heart, a scoundrel.
But every word you've ever said
and every deed you've ever done
I'm going to face you with them.
Think about this, you who put God out of mind,
think on;
A day will come when they will come for you,
and nothing on earth will help.

He who only thanks me for what I have done
has done what is proper,
and that's all I ask for;

And he who is wise enough to let me guide him
shall have a God to help him
and a friend.

Psalm 51

You are indeed full of mercy, Lord, full of goodness;
    let your mercy and goodness wipe out the wrong I have done.
Wash all my guilt away, every spot of it;
    it nags me to death, it hounds me all day long.
You are the one I've offended, it's you I've displeased,
    and whatever you do to me it will be just.
I was born a sinner, there was sin in my very conception,
    but the wonder of your grace is how it works secretly,
    and through that mystery a man may come to wisdom.
With a handful of hyssop sprinkle me, I shall be clean;
    your ritual washing will make me whiter than snow.
Then my ears may hear again the sounds of gladness,
    and the bones that you had broken will dance for joy.
Turn a blind eye to my wrongs, Lord;
    tell me I haven't done them.
Set a new heart in me, dear Lord,
    a good one, and a new spirit;
Don't be 'not at home' to me, Lord;
    don't take your friendship from me.
Let me remember how good your deliverance feels,
    how good to be strong in your spirit.
I will show other strays the ways that lead back to you,
    I will show them and they will follow.
My blood should be shed for what I have done; I know it:
    but Lord, dear Lord, deliver me.
See if I won't be grateful then;
    see if my lips are slow or are sotto voce
To praise the mercy that tempers justice,
    to praise you more than you have been praised before.
You are not to be bought by sacrifices;
    if I tried it, I know they wouldn't be accepted;
What I bring you instead is a contrite spirit;

I know you won't reject a broken heart.
And spare the city of Sion, I know you love it;
    let us see the walls of Jerusalem rise again.
Then shall the rituals have their proper function
    and you will accept the offering slain at the altar.

Psalm 52

Why do you boast, O man of importance, of what you have
        got away with?
    Haven't you heard God is merciful to his friends?
Sharpen your tongue as you will, sharp as a deadly razor,
    and teach it to lie with a serpent's cunning,
You still won't get the better of God, or justice;
    in the end you'll be found out, and you'll face the music.
You'll see your empire in ruins;
    all your connections will not know you.
The poor and honest look on amazed;
    well, they can see the funny side of it:
This was a man too big to have God for a backup;
    sure, he was rich; sure, he was smart; sure, he was well
        insured.
Me, though? Call me an olive-tree. I go on. I flower, I fruit.
    In the garden of God. For ever and ever. As long as his
        mercy lasts.
And as long as it lasts, I will keep up my singing of psalms,
    for this, and all of the marvels that you've done;
And those who know you and love you will join in as well,
    and our hope in you, which is good, will go on for ever.

Psalm 53

The idiot has convinced himself
    THERE IS NO GOD.
Men are, in the main, vile, disgusting; depraved;
    as for doing good, none of them tries it.
From high in heaven God inspected the children of Adam,
    to find just one, perhaps, who kept him in mind.
But no, not one; they were infidels to a man;
    and as for doing good, no one was trying it.
They have swallowed up my people as if they were bread,
    and did anyone think to say grace?
Now look at them, fleeing from shadows,
    wet with fear where there's nothing for them to fear.
Now look again, where they camp against my people;
    their tents are gone, but their bones are left behind them.
And in that way shall Israel be delivered,
    when God shall come from Sion to save his people;
Then you'll hear rejoicing out of Jacob;
    then there'll be all-night singing in Israel.

Psalm 54

For the sake of your own good name, Lord,
    help me, back me, please.
Hear what I pray,
    and when you hear may it move you.
False friends betray me,
    I am fighting for my life.
But they have left you out of account,
    you that I turn to, you who are life to me.
And those who are watching my every step
    let their own cunning undo them;
Let truth come from your own lips to silence theirs.
And I will give thanks with sacrifice and joy;
    I will call you good, because that's what you are;
You who are with me in every trouble I have;
    you who will bring me to see my enemies kneeling.

Psalm 55

Hear this my prayer, O God; please, don't ignore me;
Hear me, and give me your kind of answer, because I need it.
They are at my door, my enemies, wanting my blood;
In their fury and malice they plot me a thousand deaths.
My heart is quaking inside me, death knocks on the door of my
      ribs;
From top to toe I am trembling, and my mind is crowded with
      horrors.
And I said, 'If I only had wings, I might fly like a dove and escape;
Far away, as far as I could; to a place where no one would find
      me;
In the rocks of the desert I would hide, safe from all storm and
      trouble.'
Divide the tongues that are turned against me, Lord; let them
      clash.
Violence stalks the city streets, and bloodshed walks in broad
      daylight;
Scandal, rumours and mischief are all the news;
It isn't safe to be out of doors; the public squares are suicide.
Had it been an enemy who brought me to this, I could have borne
      it;
Someone who long had hated me, I could have defended myself;
But you, who I treated as equal, as companion, as a friend,
You who went alongside me to share worship together, and God.
May those whose hearts are evil, and their homes that harboured
      it,
Come to the place where evil has its way.
But I will call on my God and the Lord will save me.
I will cry with tears to him, morning, noon and night,
And he will hear me, he will set me at ease,
He will bring their violence to nothing, however many there be.
He will bring them down, the Lord Everlasting, because I asked
      him to.
Their hearts are hardened, they mock at the fear of God's justice,
They use his name to seal an agreement, and then break it;
Their words are smoother than butter, and just as easily melted;
Their promises like oil, a gloss for the hidden knife.
Give all your troubles to God, let him carry them for you;
The man who is straight may stumble, but God will support him.
As for the men of blood, of the broken word, they won't last long;

God will provide for them an appropriate mansion.
But you, Lord, are the one I have put my trust in.

Psalm 56

Have mercy and save me, Lord, from the teeth of my pursuers;
    all the day long they dog my steps and snarl.
The pack is out of control, too many to number;
    all the day long they dog my steps and snarl.
In the depths of my terror I lift up my heart to you,
    I stake my trust in one who stands above all.
With you to stand by me what do I have to fear?
    I know that my hope in you will not be groundless;
Why should I worry about their barking
    when even their bite is nothing to be afraid of?
But still they attack me, still they won't give up;
    all the day long they dog my steps and snarl.
They keep close watch on me,
    eyeing their chance with unabated malice;
They set a trap for me, but they don't realise
    that wickedness itself is the trap of the wicked;
God will reward them,
    good for good, evil for evil.
You know my case, the story of my trials;
    my tears are kept in a vial, my prayers in a book.
Each timid step of the way you've always been with me;
    it will only take one prayer to halt my pursuers.
With God behind me, I will call their bluff,
    I will put a brave face on; what can they do to me?
I am bound to God with vows and he will honour them,
    which I will repay with thanks and adoration;
For you will have brought me out of death and darkness
    to stand before you, to live all my days in your light.

Psalm 57

As mine is a soul that puts its whole trust in you
  look after me, Lord, look after me:
Till the storms are over and done
  let me hide under the shelter of your wings.
I am calling to you, Lord; the Most High God;
  the one who has been such a friend to me.
Show me once more that love that never runs out;
  come down from heaven and help me.
Your own hand alone can whip my tormentors
  and put them to panting and flight.
My soul is in a lions' den
  where children of men are just meat;
Their teeth are sharper than arrows or spears,
  and their tongues are sharper than swords.
It's a good time now to show yourself, O God,
  astride the heavens, and glorious over the earth.
They have tried to bring me down with a net for my feet;
  they dug me a pit – may they fall in it themselves.
My heart is true, dear God, my heart is true;
  I will sing, I will compose a psalm:
My soul, exert yourself, there's work to be done;
  lyre and harp, only your best will do.
I will get up with the sun to give you thanks,
  I will wake up all the nations with praise of God;
I will make up psalms that every nation will sing,
  and every land will approve them and find them true;
Because your love like the heavens will never run out,
  because your goodness reaches to the skies.
It's a good time now to show yourself, O God,
  astride the heavens, and glorious over the earth.

Psalm 58

You who are in charge, will you stand investigation?
  Do you treat all men alike, without interest?
I needn't ask. Your hearts are full of scheming;

the earth bears witness of your management.
The evil man was rotten before he was born,
    a crooked liar even in the womb;
Born full of poison like a snake,
    deaf as an adder that has no ears;
However skilful the charmer, he won't listen,
    however graceful the music.
Smash their teeth in, Lord,
    and break their unbelieving lion's jaws;
Spill them like water from a jug,
    put them to flight like arrows;
Let them run away like sweating snails,
    let them see no more of the sun than aborted foetuses;
Let them be vexed as hot as pots on kindling,
    let them be taken as sudden as straw in a whirlwind.
This retribution will not pain honest men
    when the blood of the wicked has stained their feet;
They will declare: *It's true, the just shall have their reward;*
    there is a God after all that judges the earth.

Psalm 59

Save me, O God, from all my enemies;
    deliver me when they mass against me;
From the deceiver and from the man of blood
    let your sovereign hands defend me and preserve me.
They lie in wait, they have sprung a trap for me,
    yet what have I ever done to provoke them?
Rise up, Lord, see what's going on, and help me,
    you who are Israel's God, you the Lord of Armies,
Rise and rebuke all nations,
    and punish all those in alliance with the unjust.
Like dogs at nightfall prowling round the city,
    look at them, listen to them howling,
Look at their terrible teeth, and their tongues dripping poison;
    as if no one sees them, as if no one hears.
But you see, Lord, you see them and laugh;
    you see all nations, you look down on them.

So I look to you, the God who is my strength,
  who keeps watch through the night, who is a castle about me;
The God who loves me he will champion me;
  with him behind me I will outsmile my challengers.
Curb them, but do not kill;
  let their living witness your power to my people;
But break their pride, Lord,
  drive them in all directions;
Let them be cursed with their own tongues' poison,
  let them pay the full price of pride, and the price of lies;
Let retribution come, let it overwhelm them;
  let them know there is still a God who is Lord of Jacob,
  who is Lord as far as their running away will take them.
Like dogs at nightfall prowling round the city,
  look at them, listen to them howling,
Look at their terrible teeth, and their tongues dripping poison;
  as if no one sees them, as if no one hears.
In spite of them, I will sing a song – of your strength,
  and of your mercy – I will rise at first light to do it;
Because you have always been good to me;
  because you are always there in time of trouble;
Because you are what I count on; this psalm is your due.

Psalm 60

You have abandoned us, O God, and we are scattered;
  we are broken by your anger; don't cast us aside;
You have shaken the land and cracked it open,
  but you can fill the gaps in, you can restore it;
You have laid a burden on us too heavy to carry,
  our legs reel under it as if we were drunk.
But now you could raise a banner to help us rally;
  those on your side could meet under your flag of Truth.
Now stretch your saving hand out to those you love;
  hear my prayer now, and now be our strong protector.

And this is the holy word the Lord has sent us:
  I will arise and carve up Shechem into pieces;

I will measure the Vale of Succoth and parcel it out;
    Manasseh is mine, and so is Gilead;
Mount Ephraim will guard my head, Judah will house my
        lawcourts;
    Edom will be my footstool, Moab my lavatory;
My battle-cry will terrify Philistia.

    Such was the prophecy of old;
But who will lead us into Edom now?
    who will make the strong-walled city surrender,
If you, Lord, have abandoned us,
    if you don't lead our armies out against them?
Lord, in our trouble be our help,
    because no human help is any good;
But with your assistance we shall all be heroes
    because we shall have some share in your victory.

Psalm 61

Lord, hear my voice and listen to my prayer,
    though I have to shout from the end of the earth to reach
        you;
Lift me up on a rock as high as Sinai,
    keep me, be an impregnable wall around me.
I will seek shelter wherever you raise your tent;
    your merciful wings will always be there to hide me.
Because, Lord, you have heard my vows with favour;
    you gave me a kingdom whose people honour your name.
Now grant this king a reign of long duration;
    through generations let him live on forever;
Forever in the presence of the Lord,
    forever guarded by faithfulness and mercy.
And day after day I will stand by my vows
    and praise your name with my psalms, day after day.

Psalm 62

My soul keeps its peace and looks toward God;
    that's where my help will come from;
I have no other hope, I don't need any;
    he's steady as a rock, he's safe as houses.
How long will you keep it up, your assault?
    you're a wall that's undermined, you're fallen already.
Their aim is to pull me down who God intends to set up;
    and their own lies convince them;
Though butter wouldn't melt in their mouths
    their hearts are full of wormwood.
But my soul keeps its peace and looks toward God;
    that's where my help will come from;
I have no other hope, I don't need any;
    he's steady as a rock, he's safe as houses.
My safety waits on him, so does my honour;
    he is my castle and the crag it stands on;
All of you, put your trust in him;
    give him your hearts, and he will keep them for you.
Man in himself is nothing but a windbag;
    for all his vaunting he's only dust and ashes.
Don't copy extortioners; don't live by the pain of the poor;
    if you get lucky, don't let it go to your head.
God has said his say already,
    and I'll repeat it:
All power is in God's hands,
    and in his heart is love;
Which means he will justly and faithfully deal us
    what we deserve.

Psalm 63

You are my God, dear God, and I want you more than anything;
    I thirst for you, Lord;
I long for you more than a man that longs for water,
    wandering lost in a desert, dried up, dying.
I have looked for you like that, longing for revelation,

longing to find your face and your glowing goodness.
The love you give is better than life itself,
    that's why I want to spend all my life on you;
That's why your name is always on my lips;
    that's why the thought of you lifts up my heart.
Before I fall asleep I whisper your name;
    before I get up I thank you for the new day;
I thank you for protecting me in danger;
    and for being with me in distress I thank you.
I don't just follow you for duty's sake,
    I cling to you, I won't let go of your hand.
Those that are after me would tear us apart,
    but they will come to nothing;
The earth will swallow them up,
    or else the jackals.
And the king will thank the Lord for his deliverance,
    and all that his deliverance pleases will;
The voices raised against him will be silent,
    but all who love the Lord will let him know it.

Psalm 64

Hear my prayer, O God, I implore you;
    save me from those who are threatening my life;
Protect me from their destructive strategies;
    preserve me when they gang together against me;
They give their tongues a cutting edge,
    their words the force of poisoned arrows,
They aim and bring the unsuspecting innocent down
    while they themselves are safely undercover;
They make their plans in private rooms
    and when the booby-traps go off
They are miles away, they are in the clear,
    congratulating each other on their cunning.
But God hasn't missed a thing;
    the carefullest secret won't fox him;
And he has arrows too,
    and nobody sees them coming.

Their words will always be evidence against them,
    so what defence do they have?
Men see their overthrow, and are amazed;
    they say, *There is some justice in the world then.*
The wise ones take it to heart;
    the honest are contented;
The just rejoice and thank the Lord;
    the upright give him a toast, and the good get merry.

Psalm 65

To give you praise, O God, is good for us,
    to give you prayers to answer, to do what we said we would;
To admit it when we are wrong,
    and not to make our guilt a secret burden,
When you are only too willing
    to take it from us.
A man is in luck who you have singled out,
    who you believe can take your friendship;
He can call your house his own, grand as it is;
    he has open access to you at any time.
He knows you as the God who will always defend him;
    he knows your terrifying love of what is good;
He is glad to share this honour with everybody,
    from every continent, from all the seven seas.
No tongue can tell what you can or cannot do,
    though day by day we can see you shifting mountains,
Putting the mighty oceans in their place,
    and sorting out the ups and downs of nations;
In every land men try to work out the signs
    of your great mind from the terrible things that happen;
Each day comes alive by your leave,
    and on your say-so each day closes.
You look after your planet like its owner,
    seeing to its prosperity, its added value;
You loose your rains, you irrigate with rivers,
    you cultivate grass and grain for man and beast;
It is a lengthy and a patient process

that every separate season serves
Before you crown the year with harvest;
     the fields are full of flowers where your feet have passed;
Even the desert some day will be green,
     coated with sheep, shining with alien corn;
And every hill be filled with birds and gladness,
     and their various songs of praise will never die down.

Psalm 66

Let the whole earth enjoy the Lord,
     and praise his name, and revel in his glory;
Let everything admit his works are amazing;
     those that oppose him can't stand up to him:
Men in his presence naturally bow;
     freely and readily they honour him in song.
Look at what God has done;
     look at his miracles on behalf of men;
He dried the sea up, dried up a running river,
     for his people to cross on foot, and didn't we cheer him.
His power will never fail, nor care for his people;
     those that resist him, what do they gain by it?
Bless the Lord, every one of you,
     don't be mean with your praise;
He has given you life, he has caught you when you were falling;
     he preserved you when you wouldn't preserve yourself.
You have tested us, O God;
     like silver you assayed us, you refined us;
You trusted us to be tried, to be trapped, to be tested;
     you have watched us come to the end of our tether;
You have let vain tyrants have the whiphand over us;
     you have seen us put through fire and water;
But in the end you have brought us through unscathed
     into the place we had most hope to be in.
Now I will give you anything you ask;
     yes, I will come to the temple,
Yes, I will keep my word,
     I won't be 'only religious when in distress';

Fat sheep and rams, oxen and goats,
　　whatever you ask for it's my pleasure to give you.
More than that, to everyone who respects the Lord
　　I will give testimony of how you treated me:
I prayed in my need to him; trusted and prayed;
　　and I thanked him even before he answered me;
I knew that I had good cause,
　　that to pray without faith or justice was waste of breath;
And yes, he heard me, answered and rescued me;
　　and I praise him now for his love that wouldn't reject me.

Psalm 67

God is good to us, he is blessing us,
The face of God is shining down on us,
His way is shown in every place,
His healing touch has come to every people.
　　So let the nations thank the Lord our God
　　And all his people praise his holy name.
Let all the nations be glad in their own way,
Let them rejoice that he will judge with justice,
Let them cheer to have so good a government.
　　So let the nations thank the Lord our God
　　And all his people praise his holy name.
The earth is ripening into harvest
And God, as good as his word, is blessing us.

He is blessing us
He is always blessing us
And end to end of the earth ought to give him thanks.

Psalm 68

When God comes up, his enemies turn shadows;
   like mists they are dispersed in his presence;
   melted like wax before a fire;
   blown away like smoke in a wild wind.
So shall the wicked encounter the face of God;
   the true-hearted, though, will greet him as day,
They will crow their good fortune,
   they will laugh for very joy.

Sing for God's sake, make his name an opera,
   who rides on horseback on the desert storm;
Whose very name is Being;
   sing to him from the heart;
Who is father to those that have lost their fathers;
   those that have lost their husbands depend on him;
Whose home is open to all;
   the homeless in him find shelter;
Those that are bound in prison
   in him have freedom that cannot be taken away:
But those that have turned against him
   have made a waterless desert for themselves.

O God, in the days when you walked before your people,
   when you strode yourself across the wilderness,
The earth quaked underfoot,
   and the very heavens trembled
In face of the God of Sinai,
   in face of the God of Israel;
Your goodness then was providence for your followers,
   rain to refresh them, even the desert bloomed;
For those that put their trust in you,
   that dwell in deserts for your sake,
You give them your own country for their own,
   wells in their hearts and in their prayers manna.

The word is out
   and all the women telling the tale,
The Kings have taken to their heels
   and all their armies with them;
Leaving their precious plunder behind

the old women are helping themselves to;
One has a dove with silver wings,
    its feathers tipped with the finest gold,
Look how it sits on the mantelpiece
    of the cattle-shed she lives in.
Meanwhile the Kings are scattered and blown
    like snowflakes over Mount Zalmon.

The mountains of Bashan tower like gods
    with their many pinnacles and peaks;
Yet, Bashan, looking down from your many peaks
    why do you envy the hill that the Lord prefers,
The hill he is fond of,
    the hill he calls his home?
Look at his entourage of chariots,
    thousands after thousands,
And all the regiments of angels
    bringing him there from Sinai,
In victory, in triumph,
    all his defeated acknowledge;
All his new neighbours shall yield to him,
    whether or not they like it.

All day and every day
    the name of the Lord is a blessing,
Who is our daily providence,
    who is our daily protector,
Who keeps death from us,
    who keeps our enemies in check,
Who brings down their pride,
    who makes nothing of their vanity.
I will fetch my people home, says the Lord,
    from the realms of the Dragon, from the depths of the sea;
Your feet shall be red with your enemies' blood
    and dogs shall rejoice at their refuse.

See, the great coming of the Lord
    into his sanctuary, into his holy place;
First comes the choir, then the band,
    and next the dancing-girls with their tambourines;
All Israel in this great Festival
    bless the Name of the Lord our God and King;

The little tribe of Benjamin takes the lead
    then all the mighty names of Judah,
Scores out of Zebulon,
    legions from Naphtali.

Our power is all in God,
    and in that power we shall do mighty things;
To honour your Temple in Jerusalem
    magi and kings shall bring great gifts to you;
Break the backs that bow down to the Savage Bull,
    and those that suck up to the Golden Calf;
Those that delight in war, break them and their standards;
    let them melt down their gods to pay you tribute;
Let them come on their knees from opulent Egypt,
    let them come from proud Cush with cap in hand.

Sing to the Lord, all nations of mankind,
    sing songs that revel in him,
Who rode on the heavens before time was,
    before the foundations of the earth were laid;
His voice, when he speaks forth,
    is the mighty thunder;
All power in heaven and earth is his,
    all Israel's strength is his;
Nothing can strike more terror into a heart
    than his face seen outside of grace;
He is the keeper of Israel;
    he gives his saints their strength and comeliness.

The name of the Lord is a blessing.

Psalm 69

Come to my rescue, Lord; the waters are up to my neck;
    I am standing on mud, on quicksand;
The water is rising, it will soon be over me;
    I have shouted till I lost my voice;
My throat is parched, I can't see a thing,

and, Lord, I can't hold on much longer.
So many hate me, more than the hairs on my head;
    so many, and for no good reason;
There's no appeasing them,
    not even by giving back things I never took;
You know the truth of it, Lord, what a fool I am,
    you know the sins that I've managed to keep from others;
O mighty God, don't let any that trust in you
    be put to shame for anything I have done;
O God of Israel, don't let any that trust in you
    be put to shame for any fault of mine.
For your sake, Lord, I have put up with insults,
    I don't dare show my face in public now;
I have to keep away from my kith and kin;
    my brothers never mention me.
I was your champion, now I'm paying for it;
    they get at me as a way of getting at you.
I fasted, and they called me hypocrite;
    I put on sackcloth, and they called me a show-off;
Important people sneer at me in their speeches;
    in the pubs and clubs there are endless jokes about me.
But I, Lord, while there is still time left to me,
    pray to you.
I know you hear me, I know you will help me,
    I know you will keep faith and be good to me;
Lift me out of the mire, don't let me sink;
    don't let it all come over my head;
Don't let the waters get me;
    don't let the well be closed, and its cover sealed.
Give me your answer, Lord, now;
    show me once more your love that never runs out;
Don't turn your back on me, Lord,
    not on a servant who loves you as much as I do.

Come to my help, Lord; quickly, if you've a mind to;
    you know my enemies' strength, and how much I need you.
You know what I've had to put up with,
    you've seen me praying when my heart was broken;
You've seen me humbled over and over again;
    you've seen my patience and my perseverance;
You've seen me struggling without a crumb of comfort;
    I've eaten humble pie; I was given vinegar for my thirst.

And their own tables groaned with a thousand feasts;
        I hope they dig their graves with their knives and forks;
I hope what their eyes popped out at makes them blind;
        I hope that 'what ached for love' will ache for ever.
Let them be troubled with your indignation;
        let them be scalded with your tears of anger;
Empty their palaces, rip up their tents,
        for setting on the one you were chastising,
For adding vicious blows and vulgar insults
        to him you had already injured.
Let their injustice have its due reward,
        and when they look for justice let them have it;
In the Book of Life where you write the names of the just
        if you come across theirs be sure to rub them out.
But lift me, Lord, by the hands that love to do good,
        out of this present pain, out of this horror,
And I will use what breath of life remains to me
        singing your praises, tiring your ears with thanks;
You'll like that better than any amount of bulls,
        any amount of hooves and horns and leather.
Let those who are poor take note,
        and those take heart who want to come closer to God:
He hears the poor,
        and those who honour him he will never let down.
Let the sky praise him, and the earth, and the sea,
        and everything in all three that has power to move;
God will uphold his Sion, he will rebuild Judah;
        and those who love him, those who uphold his name,
They and their children will inherit them,
        they and their children will call those places home.

Psalm 70

Come quickly, Lord, to my help, and save me.
Let those who plot to destroy me come to shame;
Let those that would see me hurt be disappointed;
Let those that would crow at my fall see my fame ascending.
But those that would please the Lord, let them learn

the only way to please God is to enjoy him;
Those that would praise his name, let them know
    the only way to praise him is to enjoy him.
However I am abandoned, however in need,
    the Lord is ever with me;
Sure as day comes, you too will come to my rescue;
    but Lord, don't leave it too long. Not too long, Lord.

Psalm 71

I turn to you for my help, O Lord; don't let me be disappointed;
    keep faith with me, hear me and set me free;
Let me hide inside you like a rock or a castle;
    be a crag, a tower, a tower on a crag;
And save my life, preserve me from the clutches
    of men whose hatred and cruelty know no bounds.
Lord, you are my only hope,
    and always have been, ever since I was a lad;
Your arms were about me as soon as I was born,
    when I dropped from the womb it was your hands that
        caught me.
You were my help then, and always have been;
    it's legendary the number of times you've saved me;
But I've been grateful, haven't I?
    I've made up songs that extol you, more than a few,
In good times and in bad,
    and nothing will stop me singing them.
But now when my youth has left me, don't you go with it;
    don't fail me now, just when my strength is failing;
My enemies think it's opportune, they are nodding together,
    reckoning you have deserted me, counting on it;
They are getting ready to pounce;
    when they do, they will have no mercy.
So Lord, I look to the one who's always stood by me;
    come to my help, Lord, quickly, show them again.
Bring them to nothing again, Lord, them and their plots;
    let them bring on themselves whatever they wish on me.
I wait in hope, and my hope will never run out;

I thank you for present, past and future favours;
I offer what I can, but I wish even so
    I were half as good a poet as your praises deserve.
There is no greater theme, no worthier subject,
    than what you are, O Lord, and what you have done.
You were my loving mentor when I was a child
    and you gave me wonderful reasons to honour your name,
Right to the time when grey hair has crowned my age;
    counsel me still, and never leave me.
And every age shall hear my exultation;
    my heart is as big as heaven, it's full of you,
My thanks for what you have done convulse me,
    and I weep with joy because you are as you are.
Yes, you have put me through loss, and through regret;
    I know the taste of bitter tears;
But you revived me, you stirred my spirit again,
    you grabbed me out of the grave, and there was light.
Give me your favour again, Lord, comfort me,
    and I will make a psalm on your soothing love;
I will make the delicate harp blush at its honour,
    O Holy One of Israel,
To celebrate the glory of the Most High
    while I confess how my Redeemer loves me.
Those that would bring me down will curse me in vain,
    but my proud praise will speak on to the end of time.

Psalm 72

Give the King skill, O Lord, to judge as you do;
    may the son of the King set store by justice,
That he may judge his people fairly
    and see that justice reaches the poor and needy.
Let the hills stand witness that his rule is just,
    and the mountains look on peace and prosperity.
He will uphold the cause of the humble and lowly
    against the rich and powerful;
His fame will spread, and shine as long as the sun does,
    clear and splendid as the moon;

As showers fall on the young shoots of crops
    so shall he bless his people, so shall they flourish;
So shall they live in peace where justice reigns
    and in prosperity, until the moon stops shining.
From sea to sea his power will establish peace,
    from Egypt to the ends of the earth;
The desert tribes honour him, who bow to nobody;
    those that oppose him grovel, or bite the dust.
From Tarshish come kings with tribute, from isles in the west;
    from Sheba and the south they bring him gifts;
Kings come from everywhere to pay their respects,
    and nations turn to him for their protection.
He will have a ready ear for the helpless victim,
    for the oppressed that no one else listens to;
Pity for those distressed will be policy,
    and he will plead their cause himself;
Their blood he will esteem, and their blessing as well,
    when he delivers them out of the rich man's clutches.
May he live long, the King, may blessings adorn him;
    may gold from Sheba pour into his treasury;
May the land turn gold with corn
    and the mountains too, right to the very peaks;
May the hills be green as Lebanon; may the cities grow like grass.
    may the name of the King be splendid,
May it shine as bright and last as long as the sun;
    may he become a proverb for all his glory.
Blessed be God, the Lord God of Israel, who alone does wonders
    on earth;
May his glory fill the world, and his name be glorious over it.
    Amen. Amen.

Psalm 73

God loves his Israel, he loves the open-hearted;
    yet my tongue came close to slipping, and my feet as well.
And why? Because of envy, and indignation,
    at how the unscrupulous prosper, and brag about it.
They never go short, they don't know what it means to scrape;

they enjoy good health and get the best of attention;
The problems and sufferings of others pass them by;
    misfortune always seems to leave them alone.
Their pride sits on them like a chain of office,
    and cruel indifference like a cloak of ermine.
Their eyes are spoilt with success;
    mad as their schemes may be they get their own way.
Their mouths are full of mockery and malice;
    no one, not even God, can share majesty with them.
They cheapen everything they talk about;
    whoever listens to them is corrupted.
Why do my people follow them?
    Can't they see them for what they are?
Or don't they care? Do they say
    'If these get away with it, why shouldn't I as well?'
Well, that seems the way of the world;
    'If you can't beat 'em, join 'em.'
In that case I was a fool all my life to be honest,
    to tell the truth, to keep my hands clean.
I've never got anything out of it, that's a fact,
    and it's cost me more than my fair share of trouble.
Yet had I allowed myself to talk like this
    I would have been betraying all decent people;
So I tried to work it out in my head,
    but, hard as I tried, I couldn't get on top of it;
Not till I ventured into the house of God;
    that's where I realised what these men would come to.
They think they are standing on firm ground
    but you have made it slippery;
One moment they are so full of themselves,
    the next they are down, with death in close attendance;
Lost like a dream that a man forgets when waking,
    like images of sleep lost in broad daylight.
When my heart was full of bitterness over it
    and I was green inside with envy,
Oh what a fool I was, what a silly ass!
    Lord, you must have taken me for a dodo!
Yet I am always with you, you hold my hand,
    you guide me, advise me, someday you'll bring me to glory.
You are all that I look for in heaven;
    having you is all that I value on earth;
My heart and my body will fail me someday

but God I will always possess.
They are lost indeed who have lost you, Lord;
  you abandon those who have given you up:
But my greatest good and my joy is being near you;
  you are mine, dear God, for ever and ever. Amen.

Psalm 74

How long will you ignore us, Lord? For ever?
  How long will you leave your own sheep unprotected?
Call to your mind the folk you picked out yourself,
  how long ago it was, how you redeemed them;
Remember how you gave them your name to use,
  and how you made your home with them on Zion.
Set foot in her again, see her in ruin,
  see your own sanctuary destroyed, beyond rebuilding.
The holy of holies was filled with your enemies' shouting,
  they set up their banners in it to show who had won;
They went to work like woodsmen in the forest;
  the timbers bowed to their axes, bowed and fell;
Their picks prized out the beautiful stone carvings,
  their hammers smashed them to debris;
They put what's left of the sanctuary to the fire,
  to destroy you, as they thought, and to defile you.
They were minded to rid the earth of us for good;
  they set every one of your synagogues on fire.
We have no word to guide us, no prophet to teach us;
  no one to say how long we have to endure it.
How long will you endure it, Lord, their taunting?
  They spit on your name and you put up with it!
Why are you so restrained?
  Why do you keep your hands behind your back?
God, you are King, and you always have been,
  your hand reaches all the earth to bring deliverance;
It split the sea in two;
  it tied the hydra's heads in knots;
It crushed the heads of Leviathan
  and threw him to the sharks, and smaller fry;

It opened a fresh spring out of solid rock;
    it held up rivers never known to stand still;
It sealed the day with the sun and the night with stars;
    it tilted the spin of the earth to make winter and summer.
And will you, Lord, put up with this enemy,
    these savages that make your name a swearword?
Will you see your darling dove made the prey of vultures?
    Will you leave.the poor, who look to you, to their fate?
Remember your promise, Lord,
    at this time when hatred and violence stalk the earth;
Don't let the poor or the helpless feel you've betrayed them;
    give them good cause to sing your praises.
Get up, dear God, and look to your own good name;
    listen to what the brutes and hooligans call you;
Don't put up with it, not for a minute longer;
    your patience eggs them on to defy you more.

Psalm 75

We have given you thanks, O God,
    we have given thanks, and bound ourselves to your name,
A name that shines with all the things you have done,
    and with all that yet you are going to do:
When the time is ripe, then I will judge mankind;
    the earth will shake, and every man be shaken,
Till I make its footing firm;
    I say to the high and mighty, Don't be a fool;
I tell the crooked and cocksure, Don't threaten me;
    for all you raise your fists against high heaven
The Creator isn't impressed.
    You can look to the east for support, you can try the west,
You can look to the mountains or hills to back you up;
    There's nothing doing.
God will judge all;
    it's he who will lift you up or knock you down.
The Lord has a cup in his hands, a cup of judgement;
    full to the brim with spiced and warm red wine;
He offers it to each man's lips,

and all must drink, and must drain it to the dregs.
For my part, I will make the most of him,
    I will judge the God of Jacob worthy of praise.
I too, where I can, will knock the wicked down,
    and wherever I can I will support the worthy.

Psalm 76

In Judah the name of God is known,
    they do him honour in Israel;
He pitched his tent in Salem,
    they built a house for him in Zion;
He blunted the arrows unleashed against her,
    and broke the bow and the sword and the shield.
Your rising, Lord, is like the sun's,
    touching the distant mountains and taming them;
The hardest hearts, that ask no mercy and give none,
    are cowed by you, they are schooled in cowardice;
The vigorous arms and energetic legs
    lie still now;
So does the horse, so does the chariot wheel,
    at the rebuke of the God of Jacob.
Lord, you are terrifying, nothing can stand in your way;
    your anger spells disaster.
When you speak in heaven the thunders roll
    and earth keeps very quiet;
When you rise up in judgement
    to answer the prayers of the just and oppressed
The righteous anger of man shall turn to praising,
    the violent anger of man shall turn to self-pity.
So make your vows to the Lord, and be sure to pay them;
    give him such gifts as you have a mind to give him;
In awe of him, be just; to whom princes will cower,
    and kings of the earth will kneel before him in terror.

Psalm 77

I cry to God, as hard as I can I cry,
    as loud as I can, and I know that he will hear me;
I kept it up all day, I kept my troubles in front of him,
    and all night as well my hands were in prayer position;
I sweated in prayer,
    I refused all offers of comfort;
In the presence of God I groaned,
    I gave up the ghost;
My eyes, screwed up, wouldn't open;
    my tongue couldn't utter a sound;
My mind was wandering,
    back to times I'd forgotten;
The whole night through I wrestled with distress,
    and lost; despair had mastered me.
Has God rejected us? Finally given us up?
    Will never do us another favour? Ever?
Has he taken away the love that never runs out?
    Torn up his covenant?
Withdrawn his gift of grace,
    and written off his mercies as a dead loss?
Then I realised: It's not his own right hand that has let mine go,
    but mine, in my weakness, letting go of his.
And then, Lord, I began to call to mind
    the wonderful times gone by when you spoke to me,
When you came to my help,
    when you blessed my body and spirit;
O God, what you do is holy!
    What God could do for me more than you have done?
Your miracles are for good, not showing off;
    though you have shown your might to the mighty nations.
Your own right hand set your people free,
    the children of Joseph and sons of Jacob.
The waters knew you, O God,
    knew you and trembled, knew you and were disturbed.
The rains came down, the thunders rolled,
    the lightnings flashed like arrows;
It was the Lord, the tempests hiding his face,
    the earth was shaking at his presence.
Your path was through the sea, through the whelming waves,
    though nobody saw your footsteps;

And you led your people just like a flock of sheep
　　with Moses as under-shepherd, Moses and Aaron.

Psalm 78

This is a lesson, my people, you need to attend to;
　　a story passed down by the wise, and a legacy for you;
Things that our fathers told us we are bound to pass on to you
　　concerning the Lord and his works, and the praise we owe
　　him.
He chose out Jacob, made a bond with him, and gave his law
　　　to Israel,
　　commanding fathers to teach their sons in turn,
Through every generation, to you,
　　and from you to generations not yet born.
He charged them to put their trust in God,
　　to treasure his words, to mind what he had done for them,
And not to follow in their fathers' footsteps,
　　wayward, contrary, thinking that they knew better,
With no firm purpose or clear understanding,
　　with hearts that couldn't concentrate on God.
The men of Ephraim, champions with the bow,
　　when the real test came they turned like sheep and ran;
They hadn't stood by God, they hadn't remembered
　　his promise to stand by those who stood by him;
They forgot his words, they forgot what he had done,
　　they forgot the things they had seen with their own eyes;
Things their fathers had told them done in their fathers' days,
　　back in the country of Zoan, back in the land of Egypt;
He split the sea in two, and conducted them through it,
　　the water stood up in banks on either side;
During the day they followed a pillar of cloud,
　　during the night a ghostly fire led them;
He gave them water to drink, out of a stone,
　　water for all in the midst of the empty desert;
From cliffs he made whole streams cascade for them
　　till they could drink no more;
And still they wouldn't trust in him;

they grumbled against him, put him on trial,
And taxed his patience to the limit,
        saying how they were better off in Egypt
And how they missed the meals they used to get;
        'If only God could give us the same out here!'
'Well, he provided water out of a rock,
        perhaps he could rustle up some bread as well, and chicken!'
God heard them, and it didn't please him;
        Jacob stoked up his anger and Israel fed the flames,
Not by their words but by their breach of trust,
        their want of faith that made him into a liar;
So he gave word, and the skies and the heavens opened,
        and manna from heaven fell on the earth like hail;
Men tasted the bread of angels,
        the very food that their hearts had lusted after;
Then the east wind blew up, and a southerly too,
        and meat came like a sandstorm;
Clouds of birds fell in dunes all over the camp,
        right at the very doors of the tents;
The people weren't slow to eat, they stuffed themselves,
        after all, he'd given them what they asked for;
Yet still they couldn't stop themselves from grumbling;
        even in the act of chewing they abused him;
That was too much; the anger of God ignited,
        and choked to death their champions and chiefs;
In spite of this they didn't learn anything;
        they even called his miracles in question;
He put an end to their days as you blow out a candle;
        their lifetimes ended in nothingness, and shame;
Others then came to their senses,
        turned to their prayers and tried religion,
Spoke well of their creator for a time
        and took some pride in God who was their deliverer;
And yet their heart wasn't in it, it was words,
        words that were lightly said, that tripped off the tongue,
But didn't bind the heart,
        words of pretended faith;
But still he didn't call their bluff, in his mercy,
        still he didn't finish them off;
He kept his anger in check,
        he practised amazing self-control;
He told himself these were only mortal men,

a puff of wind that passes and leaves no trace:
Many's the time they tempted him in the wilderness,
    trying his patience over and over again;
His saving them was out of mind,
    even his power was, and his terrors in Egypt;
As when he turned their water into blood
    and left them nothing fit to drink;
And when he sent them swarms of flies to pester them;
    and frogs that were everywhere;
And when he sent locusts to do their harvest for them;
    and what was left the caterpillars got;
And when he stripped their vines with hailstones;
    and their figs with rain; and their mulberries with frost;
And when hail struck their cattle down;
    and lightning finished their flocks;
His fury was not wild, but purposeful,
    and unremitting;
His angels of destruction went to work
    and where they passed left sorrow;
He took a tithe of Egypt, each firstborn child;
    a plague took off the flower of the children of Ham;
But he led his own people out like a flock of sheep,
    led them across a hostile wilderness,
Led them in safety, so they were not afraid,
    over the sea that closed on their enemies;
Led them as far as his holy mountain,
    the height he had marked out as his own;
Led them to lands to have as their possession,
    driving the nations out to give them room,
And settled them;
    still they rebelled, still they resisted him;
Like father like son, the Most High wasn't high enough for them;
    they set his commands at nought, and his promises;
True as a broken bow they were;
    on every hill they set up foreign shrines;
They paid for ugly effigies of gods
    copied from rival peoples;
Till God was provoked enough,
    and he left them finally to themselves;
He abandoned Israel,
    he quit the shrine in Shiloh where he had met them;
He let the ark, the token of his covenant,

be wrested from them, be taken into captivity:
He gave his people up,
    to the taunts of enemies, and to their swords;
Their fine young sons were burnt on fires like refuse;
    their daughters were made old maids;
The sword put paid to their priests;
    their widows had no time to weep for them;
Then, as a man comes out of sleep,
    as a warrior, roused, who is in his cups,
The Lord rose up of a sudden, and struck,
    and down these enemies fell, put to shame at last;
Rejecting the people of Joseph,
    and the clans of Ephraim,
He fixed on the folk of Judah
    and his favoured hill-site, Zion.
There he set up his temple to house the heavens,
    made like the globe of earth to last for ever;
He picked out David to be his champion,
    straight from the hillside where he was minding sheep,
Took him from tending ewes
    to shepherd Israel, and the flock of Jacob;
And still he feeds them, and looks after them,
    protects them, and guides them,
        with hands that are cunning, masterful, and loving.

Psalm 79

Look, Lord, at the foreign powers that enter your city,
    that desecrate the sanctuary, that make Jerusalem a ruin.
Watch them throw out the corpses of those that served you
    for carrion birds and beasts to do what they will with.
See their blood clogging all the drains of Jerusalem;
    there is no one to do them the rite of burial.
Look at the headlines of our neighbour nations,
    let their gibes and their jaw-baiting ring in your ears.
How long, O Lord, does it take to get your anger up?
    You tell us your jealousy is like a fire!
Well, now's a good time to show it to those who oppose you,

to nations that make nothing of you and yours;
See how they have emptied the homes of Jacob
    and left them smoking stones.
Please don't hold the sins of the past against us;
    look at us now, distraught, and have pity on us.
Save us, O God our Saviour, for your own name's honour;
    erase our sins from your heart, for your own name's honour.
The heathen are asking *Where is their god now?*
    show them, let them see your anger in action.
Have ears for the cries of prisoners in the death-camps;
    in your might and in your mercy set them free.
And remember the words our neighbours used against you;
    make them repent, seven times for every word.
And we, your own folk, the flock you call your own,
    will all our days forever give you thanks
And praise your name through all our generations.

Psalm 80

Shepherd of Israel, hear your sheep,
    you that lead Joseph like a flock;
You whose throne the Cherubim look up to,
    look down on Ephraim, Benjamin, Manasseh;
Let your glory and strength arise,
    let you rise like the sun and save us.
Turn us again, O God,
    show the light of your countenance and we shall be whole.
Lord God of mighty armies,
    how long will you be deaf to your people's prayers?
You have given us tears to eat,
    you have given us tears to drink, and more than enough;
You have shown us up before our neighbours,
    you have given them good leave to ridicule us.
Turn us again, O God of Hosts,
    show the light of your countenance and we shall be whole.
You brought us out of Egypt like a vine,
    you cast the other nations out to plant it;
You cleared the ground of them, helped it to root,

so that it spread and filled the country;
The shadows of it covered the mountainside,
    its branches grew and spread like tremendous cedars;
The boughs it put out reached as far as the sea
    and its shoots extended right to the river of Egypt.
But why have you broken the wall that went around it
    so that everyone passing by helps himself to the fruit?
The wild boar out of the wood uproots it
    and other animals eat it or tread it down.
Turn back again, O God of Hosts,
    look down from heaven, see, and restore your vine.
Restore the stock that you planted with your own hand,
    the branch you brought out of Egypt for your own pleasure.
And those that have cut it down and set it on fire
    may the countenance of your anger look on and consume.
And let your right hand rest on your right-hand man,
    the one you have raised in virtue to do you honour.
And we shall not turn back from you again;
    if you let us live, we shall magnify your name.
Turn us again, O Lord God of Hosts,
    show the light of your countenance, and we shall be whole.

Psalm 81

Sing fortissimo if God is your salvation,
    praise the God of Jacob for all you are worth;
On striking harp and poignant dulcimer,
    on ear-piercing pipe and spirit-stirring drum;
And when the new moon comes, as the feast prescribes,
    let the shrill horn blow riffs to honour him;
For so it is ordained to Israel,
    the God of Jacob himself gave it in hand
To Joseph and his brothers and their kin
    to bring with them when they came out of Egypt.
This prophecy came to me in an unknown tongue:

I have taken the weight off your shoulders;
    I have freed your hands from the burden of bricks;

You cried to me in distress, I delivered you;
* I gave you my promise written out in thunder;*
At the waters of Meribah I tested you
* so I might give you water and faith together;*
Listen, my people, I will be your assurance
* if you will only take my words to heart;*
You must give up all other gods;
* you must not set store by anything before me;*
I am the Lord your God;
* I am the one who delivered you from Egypt.*
And yet my people would not keep my terms
* and Israel thought it could do very well without me;*
So I let them have it their way, I set them free;
* I let them choose who they would rather follow.*
But if only my people had listened,
* if only Israel had done it my way,*
I could have brought their enemies to their knees,
* and made those that hate God's people serve them forever;*
I should have fed them with bread of the finest flour;
* I should even have made the stones provide them with honey.*

Psalm 82

The gods are assembled in the high court of heaven
 to hear what judgement God himself will deliver:

How long will you go on, judging corruptly,
* showing them favour who deserve the rod?*
You ought to see justice done to the helpless, to orphans,
* to uphold the rights of those that power oppresses;*
You ought to defend the weak, to support the needy,
* to save them from the vile clutches of the greedy.*
But you are princes of darkness, you are in the dark,
* nothing you know, and nothing you understand;*
You have turned things upside down and now
* there isn't a leg for you to stand on.*
This is my sentence:
* Gods as you are, all of you sons of the God Most High,*

Yet you shall learn to die as men do;
  men of importance, for all their pride, must fall;
And so must you.

Rise up, O God, it's time to judge the world;
  time to weigh all the nations one by one.

Psalm 83

Don't bite your tongue, O God;
  please, don't be patient and restrained.
Those that defy you aren't, just listen to them;
  look at them holding their heads up high;
They are drafting plans to exterminate your people;
  they are in committee disposing of what you call yours;
They say, 'We will solve the Jewish problem for good;
  we will wipe their name out of the history books':
On this one point they are unanimous;
  they have a common cause, a final solution;
The Edomites and the tribes of Ishmael,
  the men of Moab and the Hagarenes,
Gebal and Amalek and the Ammonites,
  the Philistines and men from the city of Tyre,
And Assyrians too have confirmed the alliance
  and joined their forces with the men of Lot.
But deal with them, Lord, as you did with Sisera,
  as you did with Jabin at the Kishon river,
As you did with the Midianites at Endor
  when they were spread like manure on the battlefield;
Let their leaders boast like Oreb and Zeeb,
  their captains brag like Zebah and Zalmunna,
Who thought to take for themselves the lands
  that God himself had given us.
Blow them away like hairymen, O Lord,
  like bits of straw the wind picks up;
Like a forest fire hunt them,
  like flames that leap from tree to tree;
Pursue them like a hurricane,

and overcome them like a thunderstorm;
Shame them, Lord, until they confess your name;
    bring them to know how you alone are the Lord,
How you alone are God over all the world.

Psalm 84

The house of the Lord of Hosts
    is home to me;
Oh how I long to be there, in the temple's courts,
    where my soul lifts up to the living God in worship;
The cheeky sparrow is at home there too,
    and to raise her young in safety
The swallow has built herself a nest
    right by the altar of the Most High God.
Happy are they who think of your house as theirs,
    they do not find it boring to do you honour;
Happy are they who count your strength as theirs,
    wherever they go they have you in their hearts;
When they pass through a waterless valley, a season of dryness,
    they refresh themselves from you as if from a spring;
If they should lose their way
    they have the Lord himself to guide them.
And he shall lead them the way to Jerusalem,
    to the outer court, to the inner, and to himself.

Lord God of Hosts, hear what I pray,
    and listen to my plea, O God of Jacob;
Be still our shield, O God, and our king's defender,
    and look in favour on him you have anointed;
A day in your courts is better spent
    than any thousand spent in pleasure elsewhere;
Better to be a doorman to the house of God
    than have pride of place in the houses of the corrupt;
For the Lord our God is the sun to us, and our shield,
    and gladly he shares his glory, and his honour;
And there's no good thing the Lord will deny
    to those that would like to be like him.

O Lord, O God of Hosts,
    happy indeed is the man who trusts in you.

Psalm 85

Lord, in the past you have blest this land of yours;
    you have turned Jacob's lot, even from backsliding;
You have set aside the guilt of your people;
    you have torn up the record of their sins;
You have put a term to your anger with us;
    you have cauterised your indignation against us.

Turn back to us again, O God our Saviour;
    restrain your righteous anger;
You surely won't hold our folly against us for ever;
    surely your rage won't reach to the last generation.
Turn back to us, Lord, and give us our lives anew;
    see all your people delighting in you again.
O Lord God of the love that never runs out,
    look down on us and be our saviour once more.
This is the word of the Lord to those that will hear him:
    it is a message of comfort he sends to his people;
He offers peace to his saints,
    to all who will give their hearts to him;
He is salvation to those who respect him;
    he will share his glory with them in their households.
Mercy and truth are met together;
    justice and peace have kissed each other;
Truth shall flower out of the earth,
    and righteousness shine down from heaven;
The Lord will bless us in all we undertake
    and all the land of the faithful shall be fruitful;
Wherever the Lord goes justice shall go before him
    to make way for his coming, to prepare his peace.

Psalm 86

Let my prayer, O Lord, reach to your ear and your heart,
    I am helpless and in need;
Preserve my spirit, for it has been true to you,
    and if I have put my trust in you, then save me.
Show me your favour again, Lord;
    all day I have been begging;
And the heart I have given you, Lord,
    fill it with joy.
I know you are glad to forgive, Lord, glad to be kind;
    I know that your love can't resist our childish crying.
So hear my prayer, Lord, listen to my pleading,
    in my time of trouble, hear me, and give me your help.
Among all the gods there's no other one like you;
    there's no other one will do the things that you do.
You have made all nations, Lord, under the sun
    and all of them will bow the knee before you
Because you and all your works are wonderful
    and you are the one true God.
So be my guide, O Lord,
    upon the path you choose, and keep me true to you;
With all my heart, O Lord, I will honour you,
    I will praise your name with joy that never runs out
Because you have loved me right from the start
    and pulled me out of the depths of desperation.
The proud and powerful, Lord, are ganged up against me,
    after my blood, with no thought of you to restrain them.
But you, Lord, are a God full of compassion,
    no niggard when it comes to kindness and mercy;
Come to me in my need, and be my strength,
    for my faith, for my mother's faith who was your handmaid;
Let me witness your grace again,
    and let them who are after me witness it,
Let them see to their shame that I have a friend in heaven,
    who is my help and strength and my defender.

Psalm 87

He has founded her upon a holy mountain,
    the Lord, who loves the gates of Sion
        before all other cities of Jacob,
She is the City of God
    and of all the glorious things they say about her
        that is her glory;
The pride of nations is the great men born in them,
    in Egypt, in mighty Babylon,
        Philistia, Ethiopia, and Tyre;
But Sion is the mother of all the nations,
    and of the worthy and great of every race
        it shall be said that he is her progeny;
And all good things have their springs in the holy city,
    and her praises will go on for ever and ever
        in songs, and dances, and psalms.

Psalm 88

O Lord my God and my deliverer,
    in the daylight hours I call on you, and in the dead of night;
Let my prayer come into your presence,
    let my sorrows have a hearing,
My troubles are at the full and I
    am staring hell in the face;
They look on me as one who is past recovery,
    as one deceased, as one already in the grave,
As one who is past all help and not worth considering
    because you have set me aside.
You have let me sink as low as any man can,
    into the depths, into the terrible dark;
I feel the full force of your anger,
    I drown in the waves of your wrath;
You have set all my friends against me;
    they decline to acknowledge me now.
I am in a prison there is no escaping from;
    in the dark and anguish my eyes are failing me;

And still every day I have prayed to you, Lord,
    on bended knees I have raised my hands to implore you.
Do the dead show gratitude for your miracles?
    do they get together to sing you choruses?
Do they exchange their testimonies in the grave?
    in the pit of destruction do they witness how you saved them?
In the bowels of darkness do they advertise your wonders?
    in the place of oblivion do they remember your victories?
I have cried to you, Lord, you know how much I have,
    and I shall be crying again to you tomorrow.
Why have you cut me off, Lord?
    why have you turned your back on me?
Man and boy, I have lived with death and with sorrow;
    I have suffered terrors, I have bowed to your blows;
I have been burnt by your rage;
    under your buffeting I have held my peace;
I have drowned in troubles the whole day through,
    and many a time they completely overwhelmed me;
You have taken away my friends, and all those that respect me;
    I only have shadows to share my sorrows with now.

Psalm 89

Lord, I shall go on singing for ever and ever
    to celebrate your favours and loving-kindness;
Your goodness is surer than the earth we stand on,
    your promises are like stars, for all to see:
I have made an eternal covenant with my elect,
    sworn to my servant David with an oath;
Your line shall continue to the end of time,
    your throne preside over all generations.
The heavens themselves, O Lord, declare your praises
    like any congregation of your saints;
Who else who walks on the skies is like the Lord?
    Where is his like in all the court of heaven?
In all the holy assembly who is more awesome,
    who stands head and shoulders above the rest?
Who can compare with you, Lord God of Hosts,

burning with power and shining with faithfulness?
You curb the boisterous arrogance of the oceans;
    you keep the seas in check, and the waves obey you.
With a single blow you crushed the head of Egypt;
    with a single arm you scattered your enemies.
You are maker of heavens, you are author of the earth;
    you founded the world, and all that it contains.
The north wind and the south rise at your bidding;
    Tabor and Hermon wear the style of your seasons.
Your arm is strength, your hand is cunning,
    your right hand is commandment.
On truth and justice is your throne established;
    mercy and peace precede you wherever you go.
How lucky are those with the sense to worship you,
    they are enlightened by you in everything;
They rejoice all day in your name for it is their comfort;
    it will sustain them in every trial they come to;
Your glory is their glory, your strength their strength;
    that's what our pride is, that's what keeps our heads up,
That God himself is our shield,
    that our true king is the Holy One of Israel.
You gave this prophecy some time ago
    to those you trusted:
I picked you out from the crowd and set you above them,
    I honoured you with the crown of a warrior-king;
I set my seal on my servant David;
    with holy oil he became my anointed one.
My hand shall protect him, my arm shall be his courage;
    no enemy will trick him, no adversary get the better of him;
I will defeat their malice myself,
    I will put paid to their mischief.
My faithfulness and mercy shall go with him
    and through my name he shall win his victories.
I will stretch out the strength of his dominion
    from the Euphrates to the sea.
He will call me 'My Father and my God,
    my Rock and my Salvation';
I will acknowledge him my first-born son,
    king above all the kings of the earth.
I will maintain my favour to him for ever
    and the covenant I made him will never be broken;
His throne shall stand as long as the heavens stand

and his line shall never cease;
Should his sons forget my law and his children forsake my
judgements,
should they lay my statutes by and ignore my
commandments,
I will bring their folly to book, I will punish them roundly,
but never deprive them of the love I have sworn to,
and never forget the word I am bound to honour;
My covenant is firm and my promise fixed;
To David I swore it on my holiness, and I will not let
him down.
His line shall run to the end of time,
his throne prevail like the sun;
It shall continue as long as the moon returns,
as long as the stars continue in the sky.

In spite of that, you reject your anointed one now,
your face is turned against him, your foot is against him;
You have put the promise you made him out of mind,
and knocked the crown off his head into the dirt;
You have broken down his walls, made his strongholds ruins;
he is easy plunder; a laughing-stock to all.
You have given comfort and power to his enemies;
you have broken his sword in battle and left him helpless;
His kingdom has come to an end, his throne is toppled;
his strength and vigour are turned to cowering shame.
How long, O Lord, will you keep yourself to yourself?
How long will you keep up your anger?
Remember I am but a man, that my days are numbered,
that all of us come to the grave and what lies beyond it.
And remember your acts of love, Lord, your former mercies,
and the oath you made yourself to your servant David.
Remember the taunts I have had to hear, O Lord,
the slanders I've had to endure from all and sundry;
Insults to you as well, Lord, not just me,
all of the line of the king that you anointed.
May the Lord's name be praised for ever.
Amen. Amen.

Psalm 90

From generation to generation, Lord,
    our refuge has been you.
Before the mountains were formed or the world came to its birth
    you were God and you always will be.
You restore a man to his dust;
    one word from you and he crumbles away;
Yesterday, for you, is a thousand years;
    in a couple of your hours whole generations have passed;
Like a dream before waking, like grass
    that rises with the dew and the dusk leaves dry and dead,
So swift is our end at your rebuke,
    so sure is our silence under your reprimand.
Your presence exposes our sins,
    you light up everything we had tried to hide;
All of our days are at once before your eye,
    and one breath makes them nothing.
Our life's allotment is threescore years and ten,
    eighty if we are lucky;
A sweat and strain for the most part,
    and quickly over;
And those that fear you most know best
    how much there is to fear, and what it tastes like.
So help us to number our days aright
    and order our lives with wisdom.
And save your anger, Lord, and pity your servants;
    don't be against us for ever.
Let your love come back like the morning to us
    and we will sing like the birds;
Let days of despair turn, now we are humbled, into days of
        gladness;
    show us, and our sons who've never seen it, what you can do;
Lay your hands on us, Lord, your gentle, majestic hands,
    bless us and all our works that they may endure.

Psalm 91

You that have the Most High as your protector,
    whose house is under the eye of the Almighty,
Who can safely say 'The Lord is what I rely on,
    I put my trust in God to uphold me in all things';
With his own hands he will rescue you
    from treachery and trap and whatever hazard.
He will hide you under his feathers,
    he will keep you safe under his mighty wings;
You need not fear the terrors of the night
    or the arrow that flies invisibly by day,
The pestilence that creeps in the dark unseen,
    or the plague that strikes men down in the light of noon.
There may be a thousand men struck down beside you,
    ten thousand maybe, and you never suffer a scratch;
His arm will shield you,
    his faithfulness surround you like a wall;
Your own eyes shall be witnesses,
    they shall see the wicked getting their reward.
Because you have counted on the Lord
    and put your confidence in the Most High
Disaster shall not strike you,
    calamity shall never molest your house;
He has given his angels orders
    to be your guardians wherever you go,
To keep their hands about you
    in case you should even stub your toe on a stone;
You may step on an asp or a rattlesnake unscathed,
    you can tread on a lion, or a dragon, and get away with it.
As he honours me with his trust, so I will deliver him;
    since we are on first name terms, I will look after him;
Whenever he speaks to me, I will listen,
    I will give him whatever he asks for;
Whenever he is in trouble I will attend him;
    I will pull him out of the fire, I will be his honour;
I will be his satisfaction the length of his days;
    he will know what it is to enjoy me, to call me his Saviour.

Psalm 92

O Lord, it does me good to give you thanks,
    to fill my lungs with the name of the Most High,
To start the morning off with good news of your love
    and to close the day with thanks for your faithfulness,
With a lute, with a ten-stringed rotta,
    with the vibrant chords of the harp.
How I rejoice in your gests, O Lord,
    how I delight in the things that you have done,
How marvellous, how full of wit and wonder,
    what an unfathomable mind they show!
And the brute is blind to it all,
    it's beyond the wayward fool to understand you;
What though the wicked fill the field like grass,
    though the evil-hearted prosper, they will all of them fail;
As long as you, Lord, keep your throne in heaven,
    your enemies will all fall and be put to the burning.
Like the wild ox I lift my head and my horns
    because you poured out such precious oil upon me;
My eyes look down on the downfall of my enemies;
    my ears hear tell of their failure who rose against me.
Like flourishing palm-trees they see honest men stand tall,
    they see them grow like cedars of Lebanon;
They are planted in the very house of the Lord,
    their roots take courage in the courts of God;
In old age vigour will not depart from them,
    they will be sturdy, widespread, and full of sap;
They will bear witness that the Lord is just,
    and his justice is hard as a rock with no fault in it.

Psalm 93

The Lord is King; he is robed in glory;
    he is dressed in glory and belted with power like the sun.
He made his earth firm so it would last forever,
    to be his enduring throne, as eternal as he is.
O Lord, the floods rose up, the floods rose over it,

the sound of the waters drowned all other sounds out;
But mightier far than the noise of terrible waters,
    mightier still than the breakers of all the seas,
Is the voice of the Lord on high;
    there is everlasting force in what he pronounces;
And as long as the Lord himself endures
    the beauty of holiness shall be his mansion.

Psalm 94

O Lord, the God of retribution,
    O God of vindication, rise and be seen.
Arise and judge the earth
    and give the vile and the arrogant what they deserve.
How long will they enjoy, O Lord,
    how long will the wicked enjoy their spoils?
How long continue effing and blinding,
    how long keep up their swaggering and bragging?
Lord, your own people they beat up in the streets;
    they enact iniquitous laws against your children;
Widows they murder, and even foreign lodgers;
    they have the stomach to strangle helpless babies;
They reason, *If the God of Jacob has eyes,*
    it's clear he doesn't give a damn about them.
Most brutal of all mankind, take heed to yourselves;
    you think there's a future in folly?
You think the one who invented the ear is deaf?
    you think the inventor of the eye needs glasses?
You think the schoolmaster of nations
    is wanting the means to correct them?
The Lord knows the thoughts of a man even while he is thinking,
    and knows for the most part they are only empty balloons.

But the man who has you, Lord, to teach him,
    I call him lucky;
Sure you lay down the law, but you keep him as well out of
        trouble,
    while the victors are digging his death-pit.

The Lord will not forsake his own folk,
 he will never abandon his people;
And justice will follow the man who is just
 and the true of heart stand in the heart of truth.
Who will stand and be counted with me against the corrupt?
 Who will support me against the workers of evil?
Had the Lord not been my backer
 I would by now be shut up and in my grave;
When I felt my feet go from under me
 I was standing on air, Lord; your love was holding me up.
Yes, like anyone else I have practised how to worry,
 but your presence sooner or later puts all things right.
Could you ever, under title of law, be a party to crime?
 Could you lend your support to any perversion of justice?
They will drag the innocent before their tribunals,
 and condemn the blood of the righteous to be shed;
But the Lord himself is my safety,
 my rock and my refuge is God,
Who will vindicate the just, and guarantee
 their retribution to the promoters of wrong;
The Vindicator will bring their schemes to nothing;
 the Lord our God will stop their mouths for good.

Psalm 95

Come on, let's sing for joy to the Lord,
 Let's raise a cheer to the champion of our freedom;
Let's come into his presence with thanksgiving,
 with psalms of joy and music that gladdens the heart.
For the Lord is a worthy God,
 an outstanding King that other gods bow down to.
He is honoured in the deepest places of the earth
 and the mountain-tops rejoice to crown him;
The sea is his, for he made it;
 all the dry land is proud of his fingerprints.
Come on, let's honour him too, let's own him,
 let's kneel and confess that the Lord has made us;
That he is our God,

that we are his folk and the flock he leads.
And let's hear what our shepherd has to tell us:

Don't harden your hearts against me;
they provoked me at Meribah, they challenged me at Massah,
Your fathers did, they tested me,
they saw me do the impossible;
For forty years I put up with their grievances
till I had had enough, and at last I said
This is a people whose very hearts are crooked,
who have no inclination to let me help them;
And in my impatience with them I resolved
They shall never find their peace in me.

Psalm 96

O sing the Lord an original song,
    one the whole earth can join in with;
A song that will bless the Lord, that will praise his name,
    that will cry out the daily news of his saving grace;
Sing of his glory to every nation,
    and let all peoples hear of his excellent works.
Great is the Lord, and worth all the praise we give him;
    worth more respect than other gods put together;
The gods of other peoples are only symbols,
    but our God is as real as the heavens he made;
All his doings are noble and beautiful,
    his properties are strength and majesty.
Honour the Lord, you families and nations,
    honour the Lord, give thanks for his glory and power;
Honour the Lord with the worship his name inspires;
    come with a freewill offering into his courts;
Worship the Lord for his beauty of holiness;
    let the whole world stand before him in awe.
Tell it abroad that the Lord is King,
    it is he that has compacted the earth,
It is he that has made it resolve its oppositions,
    it is he that will judge all nations with true justice.

Let the heavens join in the song, let the earth sing too
  let the sea sing bass and everything in it;
Let the creatures of the field add their merry voices
  and all the trees of the forest sing in the spirit.
Let this magnificent anthem greet the Lord
  at the time of his Coming,
When he comes with his judgement to judge the earth,
  with his truth to judge all people.

Psalm 97

God is our King, let the earth give thanks for that,
  let the thousands of islands in the seas rejoice;
His throne is standing on goodness and justice,
  clouds and darkness keep his face from us;
There issues from him an all-consuming fire
  to burn his enemies up about him;
His lightnings light the world in flashes
  and the earth turns pale with terror.
At the sight of the Lord the mountains melt like wax,
  at the presence of the God of the whole earth;
The heavens are bright with his righteousness
  and the earth basks in his glory.
Let those that worship ideas, that pray to statues, be cowed
    with shame;
  their very gods themselves bow down before him.
Sion rejoices at the news and the daughters of Judah are glad
  in the triumph of the judgements of the Lord,
Who is the Most High, over all the earth,
  exalted above all godlings.

All you who love the Lord, give no room to evil,
  and he will keep you safe and secure from the wicked.
He has sown a field of light for the just
  which will yield them a harvest of joy.
So let you that are honest rejoice in the Lord,
  and delight in the holiness of his name.

Psalm 98

O sing the Lord a new song
  for the marvellous things he has managed;
With his own right hand, and his holy arm
  he won himself a victory and saved us;
In the sight of all the world this was
  where he put his justice on display.
He has stood by the promise that he made
  to the favoured house of Israel,
And won himself a historic victory
  for all the world to witness.
So claim the Lord, every land of the earth,
  make his joy yours with singing;
With the harp and anything else you play
  make music for the Lord;
With clarinet and saxophone and horn
  and God in the audience, let the music swing.
Let the sea and everything in it make him
  a choral roar,
Let the rivers clap their hands and the hills applaud
  as he comes to judge his cosmos,
To judge the world with justice,
  and with fairness the folk of the earth.

Psalm 99

The Lord is King, and the peoples are in a nightmare;
  He sits on a throne of cherubim, and the earth quakes.
The Lord in Sion is mighty,
  he is sovereign lord of all nations.
Let them honour your name, the Great and Terrible,
  the Holy One, the Almighty,
The Lover of Righteousness, the Judge;
  the one that made a covenant with Jacob.
Worship the Lord our God,
  kneel down before his feet, because he is holy.

Moses and Aaron among his priests, and among his prophets
Samuel,
called on the Lord's name and he answered them.
He spoke with them out of a pillar of cloud;
they listened, they kept his word, they followed his law.
You heard their pleas, Lord, heard them and forgave;
heard them and pardoned the people they had prayed for.
Worship the Lord our God,
kneel down towards his holy hill
Because the Lord our God is holy.

Psalm 100

Give glory to God, all men of the earth,
be glad that you serve him,
let his presence fill your hearts to bursting
and his goodness fill your praises;
You know that the Lord is God,
that he it was made us,
that we are his,
his very own flock that he loves and provides for;
So enter with confidence through his gates,
fill his courts with your praises,
give him such thanks as you have to give him,
and bless his holy name;
For the Lord is good and his love will never run out,
and his truth will stand the test of all generations.

Psalm 101

I will sing you a psalm, O Lord,
to praise your justice and your mercy.
I will do what is right and be honest
whether or not it pays me.

I will see that decency shall have a home
    in my own house at least.
I will keep my motives clean
    of ignoble considerations.
I will have no truck with disloyalty,
    I will always say what I mean.
I will not be swayed by smiling principles,
    I will not countenance malice.
I will not be a party to gossip,
    I will not promote rumour or slander.
I will not flatter the tables of the proud
    or lap up their conversation.
I will find my friends among those who are true-hearted,
    men who are true to their word.
I will promote the upright, the sound, the honest;
    I will have no place for lies and compromise.
Day after day it will be my chosen task
    to clear the streets of the city of the Lord
Of criminals and those who spread corruption,
    of lies, hypocrisy, twisted truth, and cant.

Psalm 102

Lord, hear my prayer
    and let my crying move you;
Don't turn your face away from my distress;
    my appeal is urgent, hear me and give me your help.
My life is blowing away like smoke,
    my bones are like fading embers;
I am brittle and withered like grass the sun has scorched;
    I have lost the will to eat;
My own groans have worn me out;
    I am nothing but skin and bones;
I am like a vulture in the wilderness,
    an owl in some ruined mansion;
I wait and watch, like a sparrow alone,
    alone on a housetop without its mate.
My enemies are mad with rage against me;

they conspire together, they call me the vilest names;
My food is ashes, tears are my drink,
    as long as your displeasure with me continues.
You that lifted me up
    have thrown me down;
My days are no more than shadows now,
    my future is withering grass.

But you are the Lord and your days will never be over,
    all generations shall give you their approbation.
And it must be time now, Lord, for you to arise,
    for you to relent and start the relief of Sion;
Those that follow you weep for her broken stones,
    their hearts are moved to see her lie in the dust;
Then, Lord, the foreign powers will honour your name,
    and all the earthly kings will fear your sceptre,
When they shall hear the Lord has appeared in Sion,
    the Lord has raised his city up again;
He heard the prayers of those that were down and out,
    he did not hold him aloof from the prayers of the broken.
This shall be written in our history
    so that children yet unborn shall honour the Lord.
From his holy place on high the Lord looks down,
    from heaven he surveys the earth
And hears the sounds of captives helplessly groaning
    and releases those that have only death in front of them;
And his name will be on the lips of all men in Sion,
    and his praises will resound in Jerusalem,
And peoples of all the earth shall come together
    to serve the Lord, to magnify his name.

In my prime of life, my strength is broken,
    he has reduced the number of my days;
Don't snatch me away, my life's only halfway through
    while yours will last after all generations are over.
In the mists of the past you fashioned the earth's foundations,
    and you took your time embroidering the heavens;
They shall wear out, but you will go on for ever;
    they'll fall apart with age, just like old clothes;
You'll throw them away, like a cloak that's past its best.
    that's only fit for jumble.
But you never age, and your anniversaries

will never ever run out;
And the children of those that serve you, they will go on
    and their children too, if your faithfulness will let them.

Psalm 103

Praise the Lord, my soul,
    and all that is within me praise his holy name;
Praise the Lord, my soul,
    and don't forget a single one of his blessings;
Each of your sins he forgives you,
    he cures you of every ill;
He saves you time and again from fatality,
    with care and affection his arms are always around you;
He opens your eyes to pleasures you never dreamed of,
    he gives you the strength and vigour of an eagle.
Whatever he does, the Lord does justly;
    he rights the wrongs for all who have been oppressed.
He showed his heart and mind to Moses,
    and showed his power to the whole of Israel.
The Lord is sympathetic and full of goodness,
    he is slow to anger and eager to forgive;
He is not always finding fault,
    he doesn't nurse a grudge when he doesn't have to.
He has not dealt with us strictly by the book
    according to the list of our offences;
Heaven's height above the earth is infinite,
    and so is his love above all those who respect him;
And as far as the east is from the west
    such is the gap he has made between us and our sins;
And as a father loves his own children dearly
    so is his tender concern for each soul that respects him;
He knows exactly what we are made of,
    that our hearts are made of clay and our minds of dust.
Yes, like the leaves of grass are the days of man;
    he comes up like the flowers of the field;
A wind comes up, and what is there left of it?
    Nothing even to mark the place where it was.

But God's love for those that respect him never runs out;
    his justice never runs short, and it will stretch
To children's children who keep their fathers' faith
    and follow the way the Lord has given them.

The Lord has set his throne in heaven,
    his sceptre reaches over all the world.
Praise the Lord, you angels that do his bidding;
Praise the Lord, you armies of heaven who take his orders:
Praise the Lord, you creatures in every place
    that rejoice in his dominion.

And you too, my soul,
    praise the Lord.

Psalm 104

Honour the Lord, my soul;
    for you, Lord, are my God and you are magnificent;
Your majesty is splendid as the sun's;
    you are the very essence of light;
You set up the heavens as if they were a tent;
    their stable footings stand upon the waters;
The terrible storm-clouds are your chariot
    that rides on the hurricane's wings;
The winds post with your messages
    and angels quick as lightning do your bidding;
You laid the earth on its firm foundation stone.
    now nothing will ever shift it;
Not even the deep that covered it once like a cloak
    and hid the tops of the mountains;
At your command they cowered, they ran away,
    they shrank back to their station in the valleys;
You set a bourn for them and a boundary stone
    that they dare not pass to cover the earth again;
You pierce the mountainsides with pleasant springs
    and they fill the hills with the sounds of running water;
The beasts of the field are glad of them,

the wild asses drink their fill;
The birds of the air are grateful for their greenery;
    their song comes out of the leaves;
You look down on your mountains and water them
    so that all of your fields are the richer;
Your livestock thrives on the grass you grow for them
    and man on your table of greens;
He gets his bread out of the dirt of the earth
    and wine that gladdens his heart;
The oil that brings a shine to his face
    and the meat that keeps up his strength;
You give the trees of the forest rains for their thirst,
    cedars of Lebanon that were green shoots once
The Lord himself had planted – see them now,
    a paradise of birds, a tenement of untidy storks;
You give the mountain-goat on the hills his living
    among the boulders that house the whistling marmot;
Your moon and its phases tells us the time;
    your sun keeps pace with the seasons;
As soon as it sets the night comes on,
    with darkness, and those the night hides;
They come out, the lions, the creatures of the dark,
    they bay to the Lord for their food;
And when your day dawns they slink back
    to take their rest in the shadows;
But man then goes off to his work
    and his shift will last till the evening.
What you have created, O Lord,
    how many, how varied, how amazing!
The Milky Way and the molecules,
    who can tell us how you have done it?
Your sea is a thing unfathomable
    with its own strange population,
Numberless under our trafficking ships,
    that Leviathan has for a playpool.
And all of us look to you, Lord,
    when the hunger-pangs remind us;
As soon as you give we guzzle,
    we trust you at feeding-time;
When you hide your face we are troubled;
    when you hold back your hand we bite the dust;
Breathe life into us, we revive,

and the earth comes to life again.
All glory is God's, and for ever,
    and his joy is in all of his works.
He has only to look at the earth and it quakes;
    one touch, and the hills are on fire.
As long as I live I will love the Lord,
    all day I will sing my God lovesongs.
May what I sing him please him,
    may he take delight in my thoughts.
And let those that deny him be nothing,
    be as if they had never been made.

And you, my soul, praise the Lord.

Do honour to him who made you.

Psalm 105

Give thanks to the Lord, all you who know him by name;
    speak out, let the others know the things he has done:
Let your songs be full of him, full of his joy,
    filled with amazement at the works of his hands:
Be proud that you know him by his holy name;
    let those that long for the Lord rejoice in him:
Want him, as much as you can; desire his strength;
    set your heart on him wherever you may be:
Call to your mind the miracles he has done,
    rescuing, overthrowing, passing judgement:
If you are of his servant Abraham's seed,
    if you are children of his chosen Jacob.
He is our Lord and our God;
    each atom through all the earth is under his judgement:
He has made his covenant, and will stand by it,
    for a thousand generations, and even longer,
The promise that he made to Abraham,
    his word to Isaac, his vow to Jacob and his oath to Israel:
To you I grant the land of Canaan
    for your possession and inheritance.

And that when they were barely a handful,
    foreigners, refugees, moving from country to country;
Yet under his hand they were proof against ill-treatment
    and even kings for their sake were put in their place:
Don't touch them, and don't even think to do them harm;
    they have my blessing, they will speak for me.
Then he ordained a famine to waste the land;
    he starved them of their bread;
But he had sent his man ahead of them,
    Joseph, an exile, sold as a slave, betrayed;
Long years his feet were fixed in fetters,
    and an iron collar round his neck,
Till the time of his testing was over
    and his prophecy finally came to pass;
Then he was sent for by the king himself,
    the sovereign of nations set him free;
Made him lord of the royal household
    with power over all he possessed,
With authority over officialdom,
    over policy, law and instruction.
Then Israel was brought into Egypt,
    and Jacob settled in the land of Ham
Where God made his people to prosper,
    and even outdo the host nation about them;
Whose hearts he now fired with anger
    to turn on his people, to plot their downfall;
Then he sent to them his servant Moses,
    his chosen one, and Aaron his brother,
To speak his word and to show his signs
    and to work his wonders before them:
Darkness that covered the earth,
    but their hearts were still deaf to his prophets;
So their waters he turned into blood
    and their fish all died of pollution;
Their streets were littered with frogs,
    and their houses, and the bedrooms of palaces;
At his word a great cloud of mosquitoes
    and flies filled the air with terror;
He rained down hail upon them,
    with firestorms and thunder,
Blasting their vines and fig-trees
    and beating their timber to pulp;

At his word arose black clouds of locusts,
    and grasshoppers as far as the eye could see,
That ate up everything eatable in the whole land
    and left not a blade nor a leaf;
And then he taxed the first-born in all of Egypt,
    the flower of their manhood;
And led out Israel at last, burdened with gold and silver,
    and of all their tribes not one soul of them was missing.
How glad they were, the Egyptians, to see them go,
    the people who had become a curse upon them;
He gave them cloud cover,
    he lit the night-sky with fire;
He gave them the bread of heaven, as much as they wanted,
    and quails for the asking;
He opened a rock for them, gave them a spring of water,
    enough for all, in the heart of a barren desert;
And he kept the promise he had solemnly given,
    his promise to his trusting Abraham.
And so he led his chosen people out
    in triumph;
He gave them the land the heathen nations had held
    and cities and fields that others had laboured over;
And only asked that they would honour his word
    and that they would keep the law.

O give your Lord the praise that you think he's worth.

Psalm 106

Hallelujah!
Give thanks to the Lord because he is good,
    because his amazing love will never run out.
What words can contain the glorious deeds of God,
    what words are adequate to spell out his honour?
To act in all things fairly is a blessing in itself,
    to do what's right as if by nature is a joy.
When you give your own people your blessing, Lord,
    remember me, and keep me;

When your chosen people prosper, let me be with them;
    when they rejoice in you, may I joy as well;
And when you look on them with a father's pride
    may I be included with them.
We have sinned, O Lord, just as our fathers sinned;
    we have been careless, stubborn, wayward, wrong.
True to our fathers and their little faith
    who soon forgot the signs you showed them in Egypt,
Who did not trust your love, who belittled you,
    who, with the Red Sea before them, turned against you.
Yet for your own name's sake you delivered them
    and let them see your power again, and your love.
You spoke one word to the sea, and it dried up;
    you led them across where the deepest waves had been,
As if they were walking on water
    with their feet on the hot desert sands.
That's how he organised their getaway –
    he spirited them away from their enemies;
He led their bold attackers into a trap
    and the waters got them – not one of them made it home.
Then it seemed good to them to believe in his promises,
    and they sang his praises, and they meant it.
But it didn't stand the test of time, or trouble,
    and soon they were deaf again to his teachings;
Greed tempted them in the desert and they gave in to it;
    they put God's power, and patience, to the test;
He gave them everything they asked for
    till their indulgence choked them.
They challenged the authority of Moses,
    and Aaron's priesthood, and the Lord's appointments;
Then the earth opened up, and down went Dathan,
    and Abiram with all his faction after him;
A fire swept through the camp,
    and its righteous flames put paid to all complaints.
They made a golden calf in Horeb
    and bowed in reverence to a chunk of metal,
They swapped the glory of the God of Hosts
    for a graven image, for a bovine sculpture;
Out of their minds, they put out of their minds
    the hand that had delivered them from Egypt,
The signs and terrors that he made for them,
    the care at the Red Sea crossing.

It was too much; and but for Moses' pleading,
    the only man that he would listen to,
He would have undone them there and then
    and made them no more than a proverb.
The land that he had promised them
    they made little of it, they called it pie in the sky;
They sat in their tents, they whined and grumbled;
    they gave ear to everything except the word of the Lord:
So he swore by his own right hand that he would chastise them,
    scatter them over the world and make aliens of them.
Then they took to the cult of the Baal of Peor
    and dined on the carnal offerings to a dead god.
What they did there roused the Lord to a fury
    that swept through the camp in a plague;
Till Phineas stood up and stopped the rot,
    with a prayer he did it, and a javelin,
And that was a deed that brought mercy on his people
    and all generations should give him thanks for it.
They angered the Lord again at the waters of Meribah,
    and this time even Moses got out of step;
Their bickering pushed his patience beyond the limit
    and drove him to speak out of turn in his frustration.
The Lord had commanded them to destroy all their neighbours,
    but they knew better of course;
And gradually they got on quite well together;
    they picked up each other's customs,
Shared their religious ceremonies,
    and in no time at all were hooked.
Their sons and daughters were brought up
    in the practice of devil-worship,
Blood sacrifice of innocents,
    and their own children offered to the gods of Canaan;
With their own children's blood and screams
    they polluted the land of promise;
They defiled themselves with the very things
    their Lord had brought them there to cleanse.
And so the Lord came to be at war with his people,
    the ones he had chosen, the ones he had given his word to;
He left them to the mercy of their neighbours,
    to the mercy of larger states and greater powers;
Of course these turned the screw,
    of course they made slaves of them;

And though many times still he came to their rescue
    they always reverted to their rebellion.
Yet each time he heard their cry come to his ears
    his pity was easily moved;
He was reminded of his covenant
    and as he enjoys forgiving, he forgave them;
He made their new lords pity them,
    he caused them to show his mercy.

Now in this time of need, we beseech you, O Lord,
    deliver us once again from the nations that hold us;
Then without fail we shall give you the thanks we owe,
    praising you proudly, naming you heartily.

Bless the Lord, and bless the God of Israel,
    from one end of eternity to the other,
And may all people everywhere
    cry *AMEN.*

Hallelujah!

Psalm 107

Give thanks to God for his goodness,
    and for his amazing love that never runs out;
Let them confess it who the Lord has rescued,
    who he has saved from certain destruction,
Who he has gathered into his fellowship
    from lands of the rising sun and those of its setting,
From the north country and from the deepest south.

Some of them making their way through a wilderness
    lost without landmark or a star to guide them,
Famished, exhausted, dying of thirst,
    so that their spirits faint, and they look for death,
Cried to the Lord from the depths of their desperation,
    and didn't he get them out of it?
He showed them a track, he put heart into their steps,

and it took them straight to a place as good as home.
Let them give thanks for his love that never runs out
    and for all the amazing things he does for us,
Who gave them drink that were dying of thirst,
    and fed the hungry with plenty.

Some who were sitting in the dark with death hanging over them,
    locked in prison and loaded with iron chains,
For turning their backs on the laws that God had decreed
    and making light of the love of the Most High;
Hard labour had ground their spirits down,
    and when they fell they were left to lie there,
Cried to the Lord from the depths of their desperation,
    and didn't he get them out of it?
He brought them out of the dark, from the death hanging over them,
    he unlocked the door, and smashed their chains in pieces.
Let them give thanks for his love that never runs out
    and for all the amazing things he does for us,
Who broke the hinges off the doors of bronze,
    and snapped their iron bars in two.

Some who were fools and made up the rules for themselves,
    who were stricken in sickness for their vanity,
Who were even sick at the sight of nourishment
    and pined at the doors of death,
Cried to the Lord from the depths of their desperation.
    and didn't he get them out of it?
He sent his word to them and they were healed,
    he pulled them out of the peril they were sunk in.
Let them give thanks for his love that never runs out
    and for all the amazing things he does for us,
Let them make an offering to him with thanksgiving,
    and testify to his love with personal joy.

Some whose business takes them abroad on ships,
    who make their living plying the treacherous seas,
Who must have seen the mighty acts of the Lord
    and many of his marvels among the waters,
Raising the storm-winds at his single word,
    lifting the waves as high as masts, and higher,
Who have been lifted to the skies, and seen the ocean's bottom,

in peril of land, in peril of water,
Who stagger and reel about as if they were drunk,
    who with all their seamanship are helpless as babies,
Cried to the Lord from the depths of their desperation,
    and didn't he get them out of it?
A word of command and the storm sank down to a whisper,
    the sea was stilled and everything back to shipshape.
How glad they were when the storm was over and gone,
    and when he brought them safe to their journey's harbour.
Let them give thanks for his love that never runs out
    and for all the amazing things he does for us,
Let them tell their tale to a spellbound congregation,
    and praise his name before the learned and wise.

He it is turns great rivers into desert,
    well-watered country into barren waste;
He turns rich ploughland into saltmarsh
    for the barbarians who mistreat his grace.
He changes deserts into water-meadows,
    and arid wildernesses into green pastures.
He finds a home for the hungry there
    where they can build themselves a town and a market,
Where they can sow their fields and plant their vineyards
    and reap their bounty of bread and wine;
He blesses them with family and friends,
    and makes their livestock strong and lusty.
The proud and powerful find their strength subsiding,
    blow upon blow reduces them;
Those that looked down their noses are taught to grovel
    and turned out of house and home.
But he lifts the poor man out of his miseries
    and fills the table for his family.
The honest man is glad at heart to see it,
    but the selfish heart is hard with envy and pique.
So, let the wise man take these things to heart,
    let the learned learn this lesson of the Lord,
Of the love that never runs out,
    of the love that is just and choosy.

Psalm 108[1]

My heart is firm, O Lord, it is centred on you;
    it is tuned and taut as a string, and ready for music;
I will dawn with the day, with the birds that wake up singing,
    and lift my spirit to you in a fulsome psalm;
I will fill the air with thanks, and the ears of all people;
    my voice will carry your praise to the ends of the earth;
Your love that never runs out outstretches the heavens;
    your truth looks down on altitudes of sky.
Let us see your face, O God, high over the heavens,
    your glory shining down all over the earth;
And deliver all in need who are dear to you;
    hear us, O Lord; save us with your right hand.

This is the holy word the Lord has sent us:
    I will arise and carve up Shechem into pieces;
will measure the vale of Succoth and parcel it out;
    Manasseh is mine, and so is Gilead;
Mount Ephraim will guard my head, Judah will house my
        lawcourts;
    Edom will be my footstool. Moab my lavatory;
My battle-cry will terrify Philistia.

    Such was the prophecy of old;
But who will lead us into Edom now?
    who will make the strong-walled city surrender,
If you, Lord, have abandoned us,
    if you don't lead our armies out against them?
Lord, in our trouble be our help,
    because no human help is any good;
But with your assistance we shall all be heroes
    because we shall have some share in your victory.

[1] Part 1 of this psalm is the same as Psalm 57, part 2 the same as Psalm 60.

Psalm 109

O God that I take pleasure in praising,
　　why are you quiet when others have plenty to say?
They lie through their teeth about me, they lie to my face;
　　they hedge me around till I have no one to turn to.
They reward the help I gave them with an attack,
　　with accusations that make me out some monster;
For the good I did they pay me out with evil,
　　and in return for love all I get is their spite.
Those that have good reason to pray for me
　　give me this curse instead:
Give him a master who knows how to undermine him;
　　a right-hand man to store up accusations;
Let him come out of the court with guilt stamped on him;
　　let his pleading with God fall on deaf ears;
Let the remainder of his days be few;
　　let him see someone he hates take over his office;
Let his children want a father;
　　let his wife want a husband;
Let his children beg in the streets,
　　friendless and homeless;
Let all his goods come to the pawnbroker,
　　let strangers bid for them in public auctions;
Let not a soul stick by him;
　　let none take pity on his orphaned children;
Let his line be brought to a close,
　　let his name be discontinued beyond the present;
Let the sins of all his fathers be visited on him;
　　and let all his mothers' sins be openly broadcast;
Let them remain in the record-books of the Lord,
　　and let him wipe out their names from the earth instead.
Such as will pray like this shall never know
　　what friendship is, or loyalty;
He is a hunter of the down-and-out,
　　a hound who has got the scent of the broken-hearted;
For his love of cursing, let him reap the curse he has sown;
　　may he have all the blessings he ever wished on others;
He revelled in cursing as a king in his robes;
　　may it cover him like a rash, and eat into his bones;
Let it be a skin to him,
　　a tight-fitting costume that he can never take off.

So may the Lord treat all who falsely accuse me,
    all who seek to destroy me with perjury.
But you deal with me, Lord, as honour requires;
    deliver me by your love that never runs out;
You see how down I am, how broken in spirit;
    I am only a shadow, faint, and as light as a cricket;
With fasting and prayer I can't stand straight on my knees;
    I am fainting for want of food;
The sight of me has become a joke,
    it cheers them up to see me.
Help me, Lord, and save me,
    by your goodness that never runs out;
And let all men know this is your doing,
    that the honour is yours alone.
They will curse, but you will give blessing;
    they will come in the end to shame, but we shall have joy;
My accusers shall wear their dishonour
    and their shame for all to see;
And I will open my mouth to the Lord
    to give thanks before all, and to praise him,
For standing beside the poor and the honest,
    standing up against all satans for them.

Psalm 110

God spoke to my Lord and said
    Sit here at my right hand
And watch me make your enemies
    a stool to rest your feet on.
The Lord shall put into your hands
    the sceptre of authority
And out of Sion you shall have control
    of all your enemies.
They shall honour your birth with princely gifts
    fitting your holiness and glory;
From the day your mother bore you
    you will always be young,
Like the dawn of the day

with the morning dew upon you.
The Lord has given his word
    and he will not change it:
You shall be a priest for ever
    after the order of Melchizedek.
On the Day of Wrath the Lord at your right hand
    will tumble kings from their crowns;
He will judge all nations;
    the piles of the dead
Will litter the land
    as far as the eye can see.
And when he has quenched his thirst
    from a wayside brook
THEN he will lift up his head
    and be crowned with praises.

Psalm 111

Hallelujah!

All that I am I offer in praise of the Lord,
Being in the band of the blessed, all good men and true.
Can we give adequate, accurate praise for his works?
Dearer and dearer he is to us, as we consider them.
Exalt him as much as we may he is always more worthy
For the meters of mortals are useless to measure his good with.
Great is his name, and yet he deserves a far greater;
Heaven's his nickname, and Holiness, Mercy, Truth, Grace.
If those who fear him hunger, see how he feeds them!
Keeping his word for his own honour's sake;
Look how he gave his people the lands of others,
Making them gifts of cities by his own strength.
Nothing he does that is not done deeply with justice;
On stone his laws are written, and they will not adjust;
People and fashions will change, but not his wisdom;
Right is right with him, and truth is truth.
Saving his people again and again he is faithful
To a promise his people have broken again and again.

Unworthy as we are, his holy name honours us;
Vital wisdom it is that we trust him and fear him,
Wanting his teaching, enjoying our own understanding,
Yielding our wisdom to his, and gaining by giving.

Psalm 112

Hallelujah!

A man who bows himself to the Lord is in clover,
Blest with the joy he finds in divine directives;
Celebrated far and wide for his children's accomplishments,
Delighting in their integrity most of all.
Every good thing shall have place within his house,
For his own heart is a just and intelligent measure;
Good is his beacon in all things, even in darkness,
Honest men find him a great encouragement;
In generosity nobody will outdo him,
Just in his dealings, jealous of his good name;
Let things go against him, he'll never bend or buckle;
Men will long remember his name with respect.
News of disaster will not dismay him
Or ever unsettle the trust he puts in the Lord;
Patience and perseverance are his watchwords,
Quiet in spirit as enemies triumph, and fail.
Rich is the man who freely gives to the needy,
Sustained by the Lord who so freely gives to his own;
Trusting and true, he may hold his head up high.
Ungodly souls shall be aggrieved to see it,
Violent hatred and envy shall tear them in two,
While all their evil hopes are disappointed.

Psalm 113

Hallelujah!

Praise the Lord, you that delight to serve him,
    praise the High Name of God.
Bless the Lord's Holy Name,
    bless him today and for ever.
When the sun comes up may the Lord be praised
    non-stop till the time of its setting.
The Lord is over all nations Lord
    and his glory straddles the heavens.
Where is the like of the Lord our God
    anywhere in earth or in heaven,
Who though his throne is above all height
    has a care for his creatures below,
He picks the needy up out of the dust
    and the beggarly from the manure-heap;
He finds them a place in his palaces
    and makes them at home with his princes;
He upsets the quiet house of the childless wife
    with a ceaseless noise of children.

Hallelujah!

Psalm 114

When Israel came out of Egypt,
The people of Judah from a land whose tongue was foreign,
    Judah was their Holy Place
    and Israel the Temple Court;
The sea was a witness – it ran away,
Jordan held back its course;
    the mountains shook like rams
    and like timid lambs the little hills;
What terrified you, O Sea, that you ran away?
And Jordan, that you held your waters back?

you mountains, that you quaked?
and you little hills like bleating lambs?
TREMBLE, all the earth. It is the Presence of the Lord,
The Presence of the God of Jacob,
who turned rock to a pool of water
and flint into a flowing spring.

Psalm 115

Not ours, Lord, no, not ours,
the glory is yours alone,
The honours belong to your name
for keeping faith with us, for your love that never
wearies.
Why do the godless ask
Where is their God in hiding?
He hides in his heaven as clear as the day
and he does whatever he pleases.
They have their statues made out of gold and silver,
gods that workmen have moulded;
Mouths they have, but you never hear them speak,
eyes that can't make anything out;
Fitted with ears but they never hear a thing,
and nostrils they can't smell with;
Hands they can't feel with, feet they can't walk on,
and throats they can't get a sound from.
Those who made them will come to be like them,
and those who put their faith in them as well.
But Israel, you have the Lord to trust in,
to be your helper and to be your shield;
House of Aaron, you have the Lord to trust in,
to be your helper and your shield;
God-fearing men, you have the Lord to trust in,
to be your helper and your shield;
The Lord always keeps us in mind;
he is always ready to bless us;
He will bless the race of Israel,

he will bless the house of Aaron;
He will bless every one that respects him,
  no matter how poor, or how rich.
Let the Lord be your prosperity,
  you and your children after you;
Live in the joy of his blessing
  who has made both heaven and earth;
The heavens are his, and his people's,
  and the earth that he shares with mankind.
The dead, Lord, offer no praises,
  nor those that are quiet as the grave
But we bless the Lord, we the living,
  today, yes, and all our tomorrows.

Hallelujah!

Psalm 116

I love you, Lord, because you hear me,
  because you listen to my prayers;
Because you have always given me a hearing
  whenever I've asked you to.
When in the stranglehold of death
  with the grave prepared to receive me,
Tormented as I was, and in fear,
  I called on the Lord by name.
O Lord, I said to him, *help me.*
  And true to his mercy he was, and true to his love.
The Lord looks after the honest heart,
  he picked me up where I had fallen;
So heart, take your ease, and trust the Lord,
  who has always been good to you;
He has saved me from certain death, he has,
  and my feet that were going to stumble;
So now they will walk in his company
  among those who will live forever.
I trust him, even when things are at their worst,

even in bitter frustration;
Even in panic when I shout
    The whole of mankind is evil.
How can I recompense the Lord
    for all the good he has done me?
I will take the cup that he pledges salvation with,
    I will call upon him by name;
And whatever it was I promised him I would do
    I will do it boldly in public.
O how precious in his sight are the deaths of those
    who truly love him!
I was born a slave, Lord; my mother was a slave;
    but you redeemed me, you have given me freedom.
I will give you the thanks I owe, I will give it gladly,
    I will call on you by name;
And whatever it was I promised you I would do
    I will do it boldly in public,
In the very heart of the house of the Lord,
    right in the heart of Jerusalem.

Hallelujah!

Psalm 117

Praise the Lord, all of you;
    everyone, praise his name;
For his love that preserves us and holds us
    will never run out;
And he will keep his word to the end of eternity.

Hallelujah!

Psalm 118

Take your pleasure in God because he is good,
   because his love goes on for ever and ever;
Let Israel tell it to all the world
   his love goes on for ever and ever;
Let Aaron's priests in particular proclaim
   his love goes on for ever and ever;
And you that have knowledge of the Lord can testify
   his love goes on for ever and ever.
I was in trouble, I called on the Lord,
   he answered me and set me free of it.
With God beside me, what should I fear?
   what can man do to harm me?
With God beside me, what more help do I need?
   my enemies don't know they are beaten.
It's better to have the help of the Lord
   than any help man can give me.
It's better to have the help of the Lord
   than to count on prestige and power.
All the nations on earth come against me;
   in the name of the Lord I will scatter them:
On every side they surround me;
   in the name of the Lord I will scatter them:
They gather like bees, they attack like fire on brushwood;
   in the name of the Lord I will scatter them.
Under their blows I had staggered,
   but the Lord was there to support me;
The Lord my strength, my inspiration,
   and in every need my saviour!
Hear the shouts of joy in the hearts of the just,
   of gladness in the homes of the honest!
The Lord's right hand works miracles,
   his right hand raises the fallen.
This is no time to die: I shall live
   to thank the Lord for his love;
For in his love he rebukes me,
   but he doesn't cast me away.
Let the gates of the just be opened;
   I go in to give thanks to the Lord;
This is the door to his presence
   that the just man uses by right;

And there I will praise you and thank you;
 I can do it because you preserved me.
The stone that the builders despised
 is the cornerstone of the temple;
Such is the work of the Lord,
 and our eyes look in wonder at it.
On this day the Lord has set the seal of his name
 and we should not curb our joy or stint our praise.
Be always our saviour in our need, O Lord,
 be always our prosperity;
Let all who honour your name be blessed in your name,
 and may the house of the Lord be truly theirs.
The Lord is God, the light we have is from him;
 let your thanks be bound with ropes to his altar-horns.
You are my God, and how I am glad of it;
 how poor my praises seem.
But take your pleasure in God because he is good,
 because his love goes on for ever and ever.

Psalm 119

Ah what joy is theirs who keep perfect step,
 whose feet are sure in the dance of Yahweh.
Amen, how they know pleasure
 whose treasure is his phrases,
  whose hearts aspire to know him;
Aloof from injustice and pettiness
 in the figure his dance decrees;
Apt we should be to follow your lead,
 to mark your steps, to keep time;
As to that, I wish I could keep measure,
 and manage too awkward feet;
Attentive to you, my ear would hear
 and my footsteps fall into place.
An uplifting heart pays you honour,
 O Lord, it knows you deserve;
And I, I honour your orders,
 oh do not leave me alone.

But how shall a young man keep step with you?
    By having an ear to hear.
Because my heart is hasty for you
    don't let my feet go wrong:
Built in my bones are your directions
    to keep my steps from stumbling.
Blessed in being, O Master,
    your will is my safe conduct.
Be my lips the applause of your law,
    and your glory's spokesman.
Bliss it is hearing your voice,
    treasure the wealth of your sayings.
By countenancing your counsel
    I pace the paths of your promise;
Best of all blessings to know your mind
    – may my memory blaze with the vision.

Command me to be alive,
    let me breathe in the breath of your word;
Cleanse the thoughts of my heart till I see
    the wonder at work of your law.
Cast out on this earth as I am,
    don't exile me too from your lordship;
Chained in suspense my eyes weep
    for the justice to come of your judgement.
Calling the wilful proud to order
    and casting the upstart down.
Clear me of what my accusers say,
    I've not compromised your orders;
Conspiring synods assault me
    for keeping the code you decreed.
Comfort is not to be found outside
    the court of your commandments.

Dust is my soul's adornment;
    deliver me, as you have promised.
Didn't I pour my heart out?
    so please, don't deny me your will;
Direct me with only one word
    and you'll see me fly to fulfil it.
Depression has dulled me, has drained me –
    yet the sound of your voice would dispel it:

Determine my footsteps before me,
    dispose me against disaffection.
Duty I owe you, I wish you,
    and duly I study your word:
Don't let them use me to mock you,
    O Lord, with my bible in hand.
Delight it is draws me towards you
    – let me dance your spontaneous dance.

Evince me, O Lord, the full of your will;
    entirely I will embrace it:
Enlighten me, so I may see to read
    and inwardly I will digest it;
Enable me to tread in your teaching
    with steps that are easy to follow;
Entice me with the charms of your law
    from lure of all other luxury:
Empty my heart of vanities,
    let it feed on the flesh of your word;
Engrave on your servant's heart
    your promise in letters of fear;
Erase the crushing case against me;
    your sentence is mercy and goodness;
Eager I am, as ever, to hear you;
    speak to me, Lord, give me life.

Feed me with your mercies, O Lord,
    save as you said you would;
Find a fit answer to all my friends
    who say my faith is unfounded;
Frankly I spoke of your friendship,
    and faithfully; don't let me down.
From first to last, for ever and ever,
    your word is my Lord and my God.
Freedom shall be the spring in my step
    as my thought dances with your thought;
Fearless under inquisition
    I shall frighten kings with your truth;
For what you are pleased to ordain
    is a source of infinite pleasure,
Filling the heart with wildfire praise,
    forcing the hands up in worship.

Give a mind to your word on which
    your servant builds his hopes;
Gratitude for it makes light
    of all the afflictions that pinch me.
Gentlemen knowingly sneer
    at the way I cling to your word;
Good you have been in the past,
    and the memory heartens me now.
Gainsaying your say is the fashion;
    blasphemous words make me cringe.
Gibberish jangles about me,
    yet within is the psalm of your law.
Gloom gathers round us, grim ogre;
    I hold onto the hand of the Lord:
Grant me no more than this,
    that I never let go and get lost.

Hear this: what I own is the Lord,
    to obey, to observe, to adore;
Hasn't my heart besieged him
    with 'O Lord, make haste to help us'?
Having weighed all in the balance
    I turn to your music's measure,
Happy to keep to the rhythm
    your law excites within me.
Heretics hustle and heckle,
    but I hold to the whole of your word;
Hour by hour I praise you;
    you are just in every season.
How I embrace them that love you,
    that have their joy in your word.
Hilarity hallows the earth, O Lord,
    as your homilies hallow me.

In fulfilment of your word,
    O Lord, you have been good to me.
Instruct me in reason and knowledge;
    all learning is love of your law.
I was wrong when I thought I had wisdom
    but you taught me my lesson – in love.
Intense is your goodness, inerrant;
    just teach me and I will learn.

Insolent wit of the clever
    I forget when I mind your mind;
Ignoring your ignorant mockers
    my pride is in knowing your will.
It is good to be schooled in affliction
    if it gains me knowledge of you.
Isn't one word of your mouth
    worth mountains of silver and gold?

Just as you made me, as truly
    perfect my understanding.
Jovial faces surround me
    of others revering your word.
Judgements, O Lord, of your mouth,
    they only are just, though they hurt me.
Joy of your kindness I cherish;
    you promised – be kind to me now.
Jubilance follows your justice;
    have mercy on my condition.
Justly the crestfallen liars
    submit to the law that I love;
Joined to all those that respect you,
    we many, united, rejoice.
Jewels of lore my adornment,
    and I jealously guard them all.

Keeping watch for the word of your coming
    my soul is worn out, yet it hopes.
Keen was the lookout I kept;
    oh when will it come to restore me?
Kitchen smoke kippers a wineskin;
    I am shrivelled as much, yet I trust.
Kept in suspense, my time passes;
    your answer must surely come soon.
Killers prepare me an ambush;
    they take no account of your law;
Knives in their hands at the ready,
    make speed to save me, O Lord.
Knocked senseless, kicked and nigh dead,
    but still I wait on your word.
King of all kindness, O save me,
    let me prosper in your help.

Lord, your word is inscribed
    indelibly in the heavens;
Laws that you laid the earth by
    keep faith with our generations;
Lasting and life-giving logic
    that loyally follows your will.
Lost I would be through affliction
    if love had not bound you to me.
Life is the lot you supplied me,
    a lesson I tell your love by.
Learning your will is my study;
    as I am your own, Oh save me.
Liers in wait look to trap me,
    but I lie in wait in your will.
Limits curb even the best things,
    but not the regime of your goodness.

Meditating the meaning of law
    moves me to love you extremely,
Makes me wiser than all detractors
    when my mind paces its maze.
More than my teachers I master
    when I set my heart on your mind;
More than doctors of divinity
    when I keep your directions in awe.
Mindful of your commandments
    I consider each step with care;
Measured against your meaning,
    moving as if you moved me.
Meat to my hunger your mysteries,
    music to marry my feet to.
Manifest through your mandate
    the sly double-dealing of sin.

Newel for all my steps is your will,
    your word is a torch for my way.
Never to flout your just decree
    I give you my oath, and will keep it.
Now quicken up my life, O Lord,
    send word to the heavy-hearted:
News from heaven makes merry,
    let me have word from you soon.

141

Narrow escapes I am used to,
 the ways of your will are well-known.
Need of your mercies each morning
 shall keep me close to your voice;
Nurtured upon your own promise
 that I shall inherit in time –
Nothing shall keep me from it,
 nothing, from claiming my own.

Odious love
 to love your law half-heartedly;
  my love is far from lukewarm.
Other hope there is none;
 only your word can I trust in.
Out of my way, unbelievers,
 I follow the line of the Lord.
Only sustain me, and help me;
 in hope alone do I prosper.
Order my steps, and ordain me
 to honour your office for good.
Opposing you, who is successful?
 they tie themselves up in their wiles.
Obscenity threatens the nation,
 yet I trust your will to prevail:
Over all is the law of your judgement;
 I fear for the Day when it falls.

Protect me against my accusers
 if I have been just in your sight:
Preserve me in goodness forever,
 saved from the pompous and proud.
Promise of justice sustains me,
 has kept my depressed eyes open.
Poor as I am make me wealthy
 with wisdom of knowing your will:
Prepare in my heart and perfect there
 the purpose and science of God.
Publish your judgement today, Lord,
 men have despised you too long.
Pearls beyond price, beyond beauty,
 each perfect clause of your law;

Precious each phrase of the master;
  not to love them is imbecile.

Right is the mystery you read us:
  its ritual is rest to my soul.
Revelation roars from your words
  to the soul of the open-hearted.
Ravenous to know your will,
  and restless, I wait for your orders.
Regard me with your favour
  as others who did you reverence.
Rule over each step that I take
  that my feet may lead me aright:
Rescue me from wrong-doing,
  and from those who would do me wrong.
Revive me with your promise,
  with one of your whispers restore me,
Red as my eyes are with weeping
  when your law is set at nought.

So just is your justice, O Yahweh,
  and your sentences consummate:
Set right in its place is each tittle
  and jot of your eloquent law.
Sinners distort all your meaning;
  their dullness drives me to anger.
Seeing your sense is well-tested
  I rest assured in your syntax.
Stupid I may be, and slow,
  but I count on your word for fulfilment.
Simply, your justice is absolute,
  and your word is truth itself.
Sickened, in shame, in sorrow,
  your word is all that sustains me.
Season by season I sound your promise,
  I stand on it, and I survive.

Turn your ear to my plea, O Lord;
  truly I long to obey you:
To you alone I turn for help,
  to you alone for instruction.
The dawn comes on me in prayer,

awaiting the dawn of your word:
To read my teacher's thoughts
my eyes stay open all night.
Teach me the secrets of your will,
O Lord, and set me in motion.
Talkative pedants molest me
who have no taste for your truth,
Truth that your word is truly,
truth that is ever nigh.
Tell us again that you love us,
testify time and again.

Unfasten this knot of frustration;
I yield my heart up to your will.
Uphold me when I am failing
with your encouraging word.
Ugly and ignorant lives they live
who have no love of your love.
Unending mercies, O Lord,
gladden the hearts of your hearers.
Under provocation and insults
I keep me close to your word.
Upset I am daily to witness
men turning their backs on you.
Unto your will I am prisoner;
let your word enfranchise me.
Unchangeable is your goodness,
inscribed in eternal Truth.

Voices of many against me;
be your single voice my defence.
Valued the gift of your promise
above hills of silver and gold.
Vice and deceit, I despise them,
but I love the law of your love.
Vehement praise I ascribe to
the virtue your word defines.
Vast is the peace of those
who go your way without stumbling.
Victory is your voice, O Lord;
my vow is to wait on your word.
Vital your will is to me,

and your love makes my love vivid.
Verse by verse I study to make
    your commandments my own.

Wisdom is what you have promised,
    O when will you grant possession?
Waiting and wanting your blessing,
    and I wait, and I want it still.
With my lips I seek to praise you
    for the wisdom you promised to give them.
When my tongue is taught to know you
    it will sing your sovereign law.
Won't you reach out your hand to me
    that I might grasp your desire?
Weary I am with frustration, Lord,
    but I know you will see me through.
While I live my life shall be yours,
    my praise and my joy in your justice.
Wayward as I am, your lost sheep,
    Lord, bring me at last to your bidding.

Psalm 120

Up to my eyes in trouble I called on the Lord,
    and he heard me.
Save me, O Lord, I said, from lips that lie,
    and from tongues that flout the truth.
What is his remedy for tongues that are coated with lies?
    A sharp edge to scrape, and hot charcoal to cauterise.
Unhappy the exile's lot, specially in Meshech,
    specially in the huts of the camp at Kedar.
Too long a time I have lived
    among men who will never hear of peace;
I am for peace, but whenever I advocate it
    they reach for their revolvers.

Psalm 121

I keep my eyes on the mountains
    for that's where my help will come from,
Help that only the Lord can give
    who made the earth and the heavens.
He will keep your foot from stumbling,
    he'll watch over you while you sleep;
The one who safeguards Israel
    never sleeps himself, or gets drowsy;
And he is the one who will guard you,
    he is your right-hand man;
He will keep the sun off you at noon
    and the light of the moon at night;
He will stand between you and all evil,
    he will save you body and soul;
In all your comings and goings the Lord will be with you
    from now on till the very end of time.

Psalm 122

How glad I was to hear them say
    We shall go again into the house of the Lord.
And here we are, standing inside your gates,
    O Jerusalem.
Jerusalem, most beautiful of cities,
    that everyone desires to come to;
Where all the people of the Lord
    come to bring thanks, as they are bound to do;
And there the seat of judgement is set,
    and the thrones of the house of David.
O pray for the peace of the City of Peace,
    and may all who love you prosper;
May there be peace inside your walls
    and plenty in your houses.
For the sake of my kin and my closest friends
    I will pray for your peace every day;
For the sake of the house of the Lord our God
    I will never fail to pray.

Psalm 123

I lift my eyes up to heaven
    for it's said that's where you live.
As a slave's eye is fixed on his master's hand,
    and the slave-girl watches her mistress,
So are our eyes on the Lord our God
    as we await his mercy.
Show us your mercy, O Lord, show us your love,
    we have had so much to put up with;
I don't think we can take it much more,
    the rich man's ridicule,
        the pride of the man of power.

Psalm 124

Had the Lord not been with us, Israel can say,
    had the Lord not been with us when they attacked,
When their temper was up against us,
    they would have eaten us alive;
The floods would have swept us away,
    the waves overwhelmed us,
And wallowing in the waters we would have drowned.
But the Lord be praised, who preserved us from their teeth.
We had a narrow escape
    like a bird from a fowler's trap;
The trap just broke,
    and so we got away.
It was the name of the Lord that came to our help,
    the manufacturer of earth and heaven.

Psalm 125

Those who put their trust in the Lord
    are strong as the holy Mount Sion,
The hill that shall never be shaken,

the hill that forever will stand.
And as the hills surround Jerusalem
   so shall the Lord enfold the ones he loves,
His arms about them
   now, and for evermore.
A city where honest men shall be at home,
   where the godless shall never take over;
Where corruption shall never spread
   that even taints the just.
Do good, O Lord, for those whose hearts are good,
   for those whose hearts are true and their words to be trusted;
But those who are crooked in word and in all their ways
   put them straight, O Lord, and let them feel correction.
And give your Israel peace,
   and your city of Salem.

Psalm 126

When the Lord put paid to Sion's captivity
   for us it was like living in a dream;
Our talk turned into laughter,
   and our speaking into song.
The rumour went round all the world,
   'The Lord has done them a favour.'
Some favour, Lord, some holiday,
   and didn't we celebrate it!

We need such a day again, Lord; change our fortune;
   as streams return to dry beds, come back to us.
We have sown our corn in tears,
   let us reap it in joy;
We took our seed to the field
   and scattered it weeping,
But we shall come home again singing,
   with backs bent under the sheaves.

Psalm 127

Unless the Lord builds the house
    they are wasting their time who build it:
Unless the Lord guards the city
    the sentries stay in vain on the alert.
In vain is your getting up early,
    your going late to bed,
And working all hours for a living.
    God knows our needs, and he blesses those he loves.
Aren't children a gift of God,
    and the fruit of the womb a reward?
A man's sons are like his arrows,
    his strength and his protection,
And he is a lucky man indeed
    whose quiver is well supplied;
He will not easily be overcome
    when his enemies confront him.

Psalm 128

You who respect the Lord and are guided by him
    could not be luckier than you are:
You will get to eat what your own work has earned,
    you shall enjoy contentment, you shall do well;
Your wife shall be like a plentiful vine
    and the gladness of your house;
Your children round your table
    olive branches in spring.
This is the blessing a man can expect
    who bows himself to the Lord.
The Lord out of Sion shall bless you,
    shall have you share in Jerusalem's prosperity
As long as you shall live,
    and give you leave to see your children's children
And Israel at peace.

Psalm 129

Many a time from a lad they have set upon me
    (Israel can truly say)
Many a time from a lad they have set upon me
    but they never got me down;
They scored my back with the whip
    as deep as a ploughman's furrows:
But the Lord true to his justice
    took the whips from their hands and tore them to tiny pieces.
They shall thus be put to shame, and downcast,
    the enemies of Sion;
They shall be like grass that grows on the mud of a roof
    and wither before half-grown;
No mower will ever take it in hand,
    no reaper bring it to harvest;
And no one passing by will happen to say
    'We bless you in the name of the Lord'
Or even 'God be with you.'

Psalm 130

Out of the pit I call you, Lord;
    please, Lord, hear me
Though my voice is faint let it reach your ears
    and touch your heart of mercy.
Lord, if you keep a tally of all our sins
    then all of us are done for;
But Lord, you like to forgive
    and that's why we're bound to respect you.
I wait on the Lord, I wait with all my soul,
    his word is my only hope;
My soul looks out for the Lord,
    eager as any watchman for the morning.
Israel, watch for the morning,
    watch for the Lord,
Because his love for you will never run out,
    and because he has the power to set men free;
And only he will ever free Israel,
    only he will save them from their sins.

Psalm 131

O Lord, I am not very clever,
    nor do I make much of my dignity;
I don't go in for laying down the law
    or telling my betters how to do their jobs.
I think I know my place, and it's not a high one;
    I'm not so much a man as a little child,
A child barely weaned, and still clinging to its mother.
    Let Israel always be like this:
Let us be absolute in our trust in you.

Psalm 132

Remember David, O Lord, and the troubles he had,
    and how he made a vow to the God of Jacob:
'I will not seek the shelter of my house
    or climb into the comfort of my bed;
I will not give my eyes to sleep
    or let my tired eyelids rest
Till I have found a resting-place for the ark,
    accommodation for the great God of Jacob.'
We knew it was somewhere in Ephrathah;
    we located it in Kirjath-jearim.
Now let us come into his house,
    let us fall before his footstool and worship him.
Arise, O Lord, come in to your resting-place,
    you and the ark, the symbol of your covenant.
Your priests shall be dressed in albs of innocence,
    your saints of the faith will shout and sing for joy.
For David's sake, who served you,
    do not reject the king you have anointed;
Even as you swore to David
    an oath that you will not break:
'I will establish on your throne
    a prince of your own body;
And if your sons will keep my covenant,
    and uphold my doctrine and decrees,

Sons of their sons will sit on your throne
    till thrones and kingdoms cease.'
For the Lord himself has picked out Sion
    to be his capital and home:
'This shall be forever where I shall live,
    the place that I am pleased to call my own.
Her poor shall prosper by my blessing,
    her needy not know hunger;
Her priests shall be dressed in albs of holiness,
    her saints of the faith will shout and sing for joy.
I will keep alive the line of David's house,
    and keep alight the lamp of his dominion;
I will dress his enemies in the dust of shame,
    while on his head a crown of light will shine.'

Psalm 133

How pleasant it is, how good
    for brothers to worship together as one.
It is like the fragrance of anointing oil
    poured on the head and down the beard,
The beard of Aaron, when it runs down
    right to the very hem of his vestments.
It is like the dews of Hermon
    refreshing the thirsty hills of Sion,
That the Lord promised his blessing to
    and in his blessing life.

Psalm 134

It's a good time to bless the Lord,
    you who are followers of the Lord,
You who come to the house of the Lord
    night by night to honour him.

Lift up your hearts in the sanctuary,
 lift up your hands to bless his name,
The Lord, the maker of heaven and earth,
 who blesses you out of Sion.

Psalm 135

Hallelujah!

Praise the name of the Lord;
 you who desire to serve him,
Who delight to be in his house,
 who come each day to his courts, praise him.
Praise the Lord, it is good to;
 honour his name with psalms, it will gladden your hearts.
The Lord has chosen out Jacob for himself
 and Israel for his favour.
The Lord is great beyond reckoning,
 the Lord is above all gods.
The Lord does what he pleases,
 in heaven and earth, and in the depths of the seas;
He raises clouds from the ends of the earth,
 he unleashes their rains with lightning,
And he calls forth winds and forth they come
 from the places where they were hidden.
All the firstborn in Egypt, both man and beast,
 he struck them down.
He showed his power to Egypt in signs and wonders,
 to Pharaoh and all his subjects.
He undid the might of the nations,
 he did for their kings,
Sihon king of the Amorites, Og of Bashan,
 and all the potentates of Canaan,
Giving their lands to Israel
 to be his people's possession.
You name will live forever, O Lord,
 all generations shall praise you,
Who will see that justice shall be done

153

and compassion shall grace your people.
The gods of the heathen are silver and gold
    that the hands of men have moulded,
They are made with mouths that cannot speak
    and eyes unable to see;
They are given ears that do not hear
    and noses that cannot breathe:
Those who fashion them make themselves the same,
    as do all who try to trust them.
But sons of Israel, you will bless the Lord;
    sons of Aaron, you will bless the Lord;
Sons of Levi, you will bless the Lord;
    and all who respect the Lord will bless the Lord.
In Sion forever shall the Lord be blessed,
    and in Jerusalem his city.

Hallelujah!

Psalm 136

O give thanks to the Lord for his goodness,
    for his love goes on for ever.
Give thanks to the God of gods,
    for his love goes on for ever.
Give thanks to the Lord of lords,
    for his love goes on for ever.
No one does wonders as he does,
    for his love goes on for ever.
Out of wisdom he fashioned the heavens,
    for his love goes on for ever.
He laid out the earth on the waters,
    for his love goes on for ever.
He set the lights above us,
    for his love goes on for ever;
The sun to give us our days,
    for his love goes on for ever;
The moon and the stars our nights,
    for his love goes on for ever.
He destroyed the firstfruits of Egypt,

for his love goes on for ever;
To bring Israel out of their bondage,
    for his love goes on for ever.
With his outstretched arm and powerful hand,
    for his love goes on for ever,
He parted the Red Sea waters in two,
    for his love goes on for ever,
And so he made Israel pass through the waves,
    for his love goes on for ever,
But the army of Pharaoh was lost in the sea,
    for his love goes on for ever.
He led his people through trackless wastes,
    for his love goes on for ever.
He overthrew opposing kings,
    for his love goes on for ever,
Kings and their armies he put down,
    for his love goes on for ever;
Sihon king of the Amorites,
    for his love goes on for ever,
And Og, king of Bashan,
    for his love goes on for ever.
He gave their lands to Israel,
    for his love goes on for ever,
To his chosen Israel to have and to hold,
    for his love goes on for ever.
He kept us in mind when we were oppressed,
    for his love goes on for ever,
And saved us out of our enemies' hands,
    for his love goes on for ever.
He gives to all his creatures their food,
    for his love goes on for ever.
O give thanks from the heart to the God of heaven,
    for his love goes on for ever.

Psalm 137

Whenever our hearts remembered Sion
    we drowned our tears in the waters of Babylon.
We hung our harps up in the willow trees

to hide them from our hosts;
For they expected music and song from us,
 those who had forced us into exile;
'Come on,' they said, 'give us one of your tunes;
 sing us one of the songs of Sion!'
How could we sing them one of the songs of God
 with God and our land taken from us?
If I forget you, O Jerusalem,
 may my right hand be unstringed;
If I do not treasure you in my heart
 let my tongue forget how to speak;
If I do not value Jerusalem
 more than my life itself.
Remember the people of Edom, Lord,
 on the day Jerusalem fell;
Remember them shouting, 'Knock it down,
 don't leave one stone on another!'
O Babylon, proud and pitiless queen,
 blessed be he who pays you in kind for your rapine;
Blessed be he who plucks your babes from your arms
 and beats their brains out against your broken walls.

Psalm 138

I give you my thanks, O Lord, with all my heart I do;
 I praise you, as all the angels in heaven can witness.
Gladly I bow down towards your altar, to your sanctuary,
 and gladly I write your name in letters of love;
For your mercy and goodness are wider than the heavens,
 and the word you give is truth itself.
I called on you, and graciously you answered;
 you filled my heart with courage and enterprise.
The kings of the nations shall come to praise you, Lord;
 they have heard your word, they have seen what you
  can do;
They shall sing your praises, they shall confess your glory;
 they will acknowledge for all the world to hear
That though the Lord is Highest he cares for the lowly;

when the time is ripe he humiliates the proud.
Freely I walk among felons with you to protect me,
  your right hand saves me from my enemies.
With the Lord's help I shall finish the work I started;
  your love, O Lord, goes on for ever and ever,
And you will not forsake us or see us confounded,
  we who are the work of your own hands.

Psalm 139

O Lord, you made me, you know me through and through;
  you know when I have sat down, when I will stand up;
You do not need to be here to know what I'm thinking;
  you know where I'm going, you know where I will stop;
You know my disposition and my habits;
  you know what I will say before I say it;
You have walked before me, you have walked behind,
  over my head your caring hand protects me;
How much you know I simply find amazing,
  it's altogether too much for me to take in.
Where can I go where your spirit will not be with me?
  Where can I hide where you will not be present?
You are there if I fly to heaven;
  if I go to hell I shall find you there before me.
If I could fly through the dawn or through the sunset,
  forwards or backwards through time,
I wouldn't escape you, I would still be in your hands.
  If I thought to hide in the dark, to live in the night,
The dark isn't dark to you, the night isn't night;
  To your eyes light and dark are much the same.
You were there presiding as my being was fashioned,
  as in my mother's womb my flesh was formed;
I was fearfully and wonderfully made
  like all your creatures, and I praise you for it;
Before I ever was you knew me,
  just who and what I am you've known from then,
How I developed cell by cell in secret,
  how the unknown programme of genes revealed itself.

You saw the stalks of my primitive limbs in the womb
    – it's all recorded in your memory –
As day by day creation was in process
    and step by step the stages took their turn.
Your mind, O God, is far too deep for my reason,
    your thoughts so far beyond my estimating.
Are they computable? Might as well count the sands,
    I'd need a life as long as yours to do it.
If only, God, if only you'd wipe out the wicked!
    If only we could be free of the bloodthirsty sods!
Those who defy you with deliberate evil,
    those who despise you and spit on your very name.
Oh how I hate them, Lord, because they hate you!
    It makes me sick to see them get away with it.
I hate them with a hatred that will not dwindle,
    I hate them from my soul as enemies.
But test me, Lord, and scrutinise my heart;
    I want your understanding, and your guidance;
And keep an eye on me so I don't offend you,
    and with your ageless wisdom guide me still.

Psalm 140

Save me, Lord, from those who do not hate evil;
    protect me from those who yield to their violent hearts,
Who contemplate wrong, who plan it,
    who are in their element causing trouble.
Their tongues are as sharp as serpents' fangs.
    their lips are coated with poison.
Save me, Lord, from the wicked man's power,
    protect me from those who want to wipe me out.
They lay their snares, they spread their nets,
    they set their booby traps.
So I prayed: 'O Lord, you are my God,
    hear my plea and have mercy.
You are my only safety, Lord,
    you are my helmet and shield.
You know their designs against me, Lord;

stop them, don't let them always have their way.
Let the mouths that opened to undo me
    speak to their own undoing;
Let red-hot coals fall on their heads,
    let them fall in some muddy hole they can't get out of.
Let slander find no ear to make its home in;
    and let evil and violence come to a violent end.'
I know the Lord will give the needy their due,
    and justice to the oppressed;
And honest men will speak your name with thanksgiving,
    with worship, which is simply applauding your presence.

Psalm 141

O Lord, come quickly, hear my cry for help;
    don't let my words and tears be spent in vain;
Let my prayer rise up to you as incense rises;
    let my lifted hands be a welcome sacrifice.
Let a guard be posted on my lips, O Lord,
    to keep my mouth from malice.
Arrest my heart if it strays to evil thoughts,
    and chain my feet if they want to follow folly.
Let the corrupt want my company in vain,
    let not their tables tempt me;
I'd rather be berated by the honest,
    and get a hearty wigging from those I respect.
I will keep myself from the ceremonies of the top dogs
    and never be party to their code of honour;
Though they tried to soften justice it's hard as a rock
    as they will find, and I will have told them so.
Like clods of earth the harrow has broken small
    their scattered bones will litter the ground they fell on.
But on you, O Lord my God, I have fixed my eyes;
    you are my help, you are my sole protection.
Keep me out of the trap they have set for me,
    let all their wiles be wasted.
May their devices go off in their own faces
    while I pass by unscathed.

Psalm 142

I cry to the Lord, loudly I call upon him;
  I pour all my troubles out to him in abandon.
When my courage is come to an end
  you are here beside me.
You know the way I should go,
  you know where their traps are.
At my right hand I have no friend to count on,
  and no escape in sight, no rescue to hope for.
So I cry to you, Lord,
  I tell you 'You are my refuge;
You're all that I have
  in this life and any other.
Hear what I ask, as I ask it in desperation:
  save me from those who are hunting me, Oh so many!
Just get me out of this hole
  and I'll praise you for ever,
With all who are loyal as well
  giving thanks for your favour.'

Psalm 143

Lord, hear my prayer, as you are faithful hear me,
  as you love justice listen to my plea;
But not as a judge armed with the rigour of law,
  since in that case there's not a man living could face you.
You know my oppressor hounds me, has ground me down,
  has darkened things so much I wish I were dead;
You know how depressed I am,
  I try to pick myself up but it doesn't work.
I dwell on the past, the prayers you answered,
  I call to mind the wonders your hands have done.
I lift my open hands to you, to fill them;
  I am a waste land that pleads with you for water.
Hear me, Lord, before it's too late;
  don't turn away and leave me to sink or swim;
Let me see your love again with the light of the morning,

as much as I have put my trust in you.
I have made my heart an empty sheet before you
    for you to write on; tell me what to do.
Save me from them, Lord;
    I am counting on you.
As you alone are my God, let me know your pleasure;
    let your spirit light up the road you have set before me.
For your own name's sake, Lord, save me;
    save those who honour you, who turn to you for justice.
And as you love me, spare me my enemies' triumph;
    and as I serve you, deal with your servant's tormentors.

Psalm 144

I bless the Lord who is a rock to me,
    who puts the fight in my hands, and flair in my fingers;
He is a help that never fails,
    a fortress that will never fall;
A shield, invisible but trustworthy,
    and as he has given me rule he will give me power.
Why is it, Lord, that you care so much about man,
    that you spare such thought for Adam and his kin?
Like the wind he is here today and gone tomorrow,
    his time no more than a shadow on a sun-dial.
But you, Lord, can knock the stars out of their courses,
    your little finger can set the mountains on fire;
When you take the battlefield your arrows are lightnings;
    every one hits its mark and doesn't just wound.
Now reach your hand from heaven to rescue me
    from the overwhelming flood of my enemies;
They are armed with lies,
    they are trained in deceit and corruption.
And O my God, I will compose you an anthem
    the like of which was never heard before
In praise of the God that kings sue to for victory,
    the God who delivered David who trusted in him.
Save me then, Lord, from the swords that are turned against me,
    from the plots of those who have got their hands on power,

Who are armed with lies,
    who are trained in deceit and corruption.
And our sons will grow up like trees, stately and sturdy,
    and our daughters upright and clean as temple columns;
Our barns will never be short of what they were built for;
    our sheep will fill the fields with lambs in thousands;
Our cattle calve without miscarriage,
    and never a war or an exile or cries in our streets.
A people that thrives like this, men call them lucky;
    they are lucky indeed who have the Lord for their God.

Psalm 145

Allworthy God, I honour you as my king,
    and as long as I have breath it will praise your name;
Be my days many or few, each one will bless you,
    each one be a holy day as I give it to you;
Can anyone overpraise the Lord,
    can anyone exaggerate his greatness?
Don't his miracles simply astonish us,
    don't witnesses find it hard to make others believe in them?
Essentially my theme is one and the same,
    your glory that is hidden in private knowledge;
For all that your public displays of saving power
    fill men with awe and profitable fear,
Grateful and humble hearts keep their gladness close
    and treasure the infinite goodness you graced them with.
He is gracious, they know, he is considerate,
    he is patient, he is kind beyond compare;
Isn't he everyone's God, and his love
    available to all his beloved creatures?
Justly, O Lord, your creatures who know you praise you,
    rightly they fInd in you a blessing each day;
Let them enlarge their language to talk of your glory,
    let them tell their own tale,
Making no bones about what they know of you,
    you and your Majesty, you and your dearest Mercy;
Not to diminish with anger, not to decline with age,

162

no, your goodness is faultless, and your mercy is perfect.
Oh how true to his word he is, how reliable;
    once he has given a promise then count it fulfilled;
Perhaps you will trip, maybe fall, he will help you up;
    perhaps be depressed, he will help you get out of it.
Quail they do not who look to you, Lord, in hope,
    and sure enough you stead them in your season,
Ready and bountiful and providential
    you give your living creatures what they need.
See if he isn't just in all his ways,
    see if he isn't true to his every word;
Try him and see, come close as you dare to him,
    and if you are straight with him he will show you his love.
Up to your eyes in worry, just ask for his help;
    be honest with him, be frank, and he will respect you.
Vicious and oily souls have good cause to fear him,
    but those who respect him he will account his own.
Which is why I have good reason to praise the Lord,
    and why we should all bless his name for ever and ever.

Psalm 146

Hallelujah!

Praise the Lord, my soul,
    praise him as long as breath remains,
Praise God with psalms as long as your being lasts.
It's useless to trust in ministers, or any man;
    they have no power to help;
They too when their time comes will surrender their breath;
    they will come to dust, and what can they do for you then?
But he whose helper and friend is the God of Jacob
    is really in luck; whose hope is in the Lord,
The one who has to his credit the whole creation,
    heavens and earth and seas and everything else;
Who is true to his promises,
    who guarantees his justice to the just,
Who is bread to the hungry,

who is freedom to the enchained;
Who is sight to the blind,
who bears the cross of the burdened,
Who is ever the friend of innocence,
who is the foreigner's protector;
Who is the champion of orphan and widow,
who brings the double-dealer to final audit.
He is the Lord and his reign shall last for ever;
he is your God, O Sion, and always will be.

Hallelujah!

Psalm 147

Hallelujah!

It does you good to sing to God,
there is no completer pleasure.
The Lord is working on Jerusalem,
he is calling the exiles home;
He is comforting the broken-spirited,
he is bandaging up the wounded;
He is calling the register of the stars,
he knows every one by name;
Our God is amazing, his power is tremendous,
and his wisdom is equal to every challenge;
He is always ready to lift the downcast up,
and ready to put the upstart down.

Sing your thanks to the Lord in song,
outdo yourself in his honour.
He covers the sky with a coat of clouds
and distils good rain for the ground;
He colours the hills with delightful grass,
and the social table with greens;
He gives his cattle their fill of food,
and even the raven, he never goes short;
He is unimpressed by the horseman's skill

or the man of war's gymnastics;
    His favour goes to the wise in heart,
        and his love to lovers of mercy.

Praise God, O Jerusalem;
    Sion, sing to the Lord,
Who has made your gates to withatand assault
    and your children to live in peace;
Who has put an end to relentless wars
    so the good wheat may wave its wealth;
His word encompasses the earth,
    swifter than satellites, or light itself;
He summons his snow and it falls like wool,
    his hoar-frost stiffens the grass,
Turns liquid drops to feathers of crystal,
    and rivers to roads of ice;
One word from him and their hardness melts,
    and warm winds release the waters.
To Jacob he has given his word,
    to Israel his commandments;
And no other nation can say the same.
    Hallelujah!

Psalm 148

Hallelujah!

Praise the Lord, you who are there in heaven,
    praise him, you who live on high;
Praise him, you who are angels of his,
    praise him, you of his battalion;
Praise him, you who are his sun and moon,
    praise him, you scintillating stars;
Praise him, you heavens and upper heavens,
    praise him, you waters that swirl beyond the heavens.
All of you, praise the Lord and bless his name
    since by his spoken word you came into being,

Ordaining you to be, for ever and ever,
    by a word no power that be can ever gainsay.

Praise the Lord, you who are there on earth,
    you oceans, and you strange creatures of the deep;
Frost and fire and mist and hail and snow,
    tempests and hurricanes that he calls up;
You his beloved mountains and his hills,
    his trees of fruit, his cedars;
His creatures of the wild, his breeding cattle,
    creatures that creep on the earth, that fly in the air;
His kings and peoples all the world over,
    you that make judgements, you that make decisions;
You who are full of youth,
    you who are children, you who are full of years;
All of us, let us praise the Lord by name;
    whose name is high above all other names;
Whose majesty both heaven and earth acknowledge.
And he has exalted his people,
    and given us power,
And crowned the ones that would serve him
    with honour and praise,
The ones who love him,
    the ones who are his Israel.

Hallelujah!

Psalm 149

Hallelujah!

Sing a new song to the Lord,
    a song of praise for the church of the saints;
A song to their Maker that Israel can sing,
    a song to their King for the children of Sion.
Let them praise him in the pattern and the vigour of the dance;
    with carol and harp and tambourine.
The Lord delights in his people's delight,

and their sorrow he crowns with salvation.
Let all exult in him as much as they love him,
    when they kneel before him let them weep for joy.
Let the praise of God be ever upon their lips,
    let it be as a two-edged sword ever in their hands
To take the nations to task,
    to challenge the heretic,
To tie their leaders in knots,
    to confound their confuters;
And to execute the sentence their enemies passed
    on those who passed it:
This is the glory,
    this is the power of praise!

Hallelujah!

Psalm 150

(first version)

Hallelujah!

Be cheerful in the Lord, be hale in his holiness;
    be strong in the potential of his power.
Revel in what he has done;
    be magnified in his magnificence.
Blow his praises on ramshorns;
    sing up with harp and guitar.
Dance for him to the tambourine;
    cheer him with woodwind and strings.
Startle him with a clash of cymbals;
    soothe him with delicate bells:
For everything that breathes is praising God;
    but us, we do it willingly.

Hallelujah!

(second version)

Hallelujah!

O praise God: in the holy chancel of his love,
      in the mighty nave of his creation.
O praise God: for all his intricate artefacts,
      for all his grandeur of design.
O praise God: sound his name with brass,
      pick it out on harpstrings.
O praise God: write it with dancing in the dust,
      sign it with flutenotes on wind.
O praise God: on cymbals wake the dead with it;
      transmit it through all outer space;
    every drawn breath speaks his honour.

Hallelujah!

Afterword

The classical languages are still taken to be Latin and Greek; and when T. S. Eliot in 1942 spoke on 'The Classics and the Man of Letters' he fell in with that assumption – naturally enough, since he was giving the presidential address to the Classical Association. Even today that Graeco-Roman bias is so strong that some may think it odd and provoking to have the Psalms of David proposed as 'a classic', just like the *Iliad* of Homer or the odes of Horace. These ancient Hebrew poems are indeed, it may be conceded, still alive and fructifying in English-language communities, but hardly in the circles that Eliot pointed to when (using an expression already obsolescent) he invoked 'the man of letters'. The Psalms undoubtedly matter still, not less in 1994 than in 1942, but mostly they matter in circles that would not be called, nor would wish to be called, 'literary'.

Gordon Jackson however, though as it happens he's a devout Christian, is every inch a man of letters; and he deals with these ancient poems as a man concerned with, and practising with distinction, the writing of poems in the English of his own day. That day is not Eliot's day; nor is it altogether mine. At the risk of misrepresenting him, I may call him a child of the 1960s. The ferment of that decade, so often and justly reprehended as destructive and self-indulgent, in certain restricted circles (mostly in and around Cambridge) took the form of a searching scrutiny of the modes and conventions which at that time dominated verse-writing in English; and, following from that, a costly strategy for bypassing the metropolitan publishing circuits in which those modes and conventions held sway. Jackson's founding of the Grosseteste Press – an enterprise which, as a young family man in Lincoln, he soon from economic necessity had to cede to others – was a rash and altruistic endeavour typical of the late 1960s at their best. His appropriate place therefore, as one who honoured as his first mentor the poet John Riley (who had not long to live), was with the writers who belatedly acceded to commercial publication in the Carcanet anthology, *A Various Art* (1987), edited by Andrew Crozier and Tim Longville. But Jackson was signally absent from that collection. Though the art which those anthologists represented was professedly 'various', a Christian art like Jackson's (who had formally become Christian in 1968) was one variety that it seems they could not easily recognize. In this they were at one with the commercial publishers to whom, in other respects, they

169

meant to offer a stringent alternative. In modern Britain Christian belief, and poems embodying that belief, are viewed askance by Establishment and anti-Establishment alike.

'Artist' is certainly the word for Jackson, rather than simply 'poet'. In this he makes common cause with David Jones, whom he is glad to recognize as one of his masters, though in matters of prosody he is harder on himself than Jones ever was. (Jackson's verse may be read as 'free', though in fact its staple is normally a line of nine syllables.) Each of his many slim books, all limited editions from his domestic workshop which trades as Asgill Press, is elaborately designed as an object to please the eye as well as the ear – and not merely to please, but also to signify in that extra dimension. His son Paul, an intricately gifted draughtsman, collaborates with him in this, to an extent that goes far beyond what is usually meant by 'illustrator'. Accordingly Jackson can hardly resent his exclusion, largely self-sought in any case, from the usual circuits of publishing; by so excluding himself he has been able to make each of his books into what Chaucer might have recognized as 'a boke': a cherished artifact fashioned entirely to his liking, as much in typeface and binding as in 'content'. And that content is itself very often a celebration of arts and artists, as in *Five Sisters York* (1980) which is in part an enraptured appreciation of the glaziers and masons of York Minster, as the more ambitious *Akropolis* (1987) describes the spiritual presence of a great church like Lincoln Cathedral as simply the transposition into another key of the physical presence that architects, with pious planners and patrons, have made of it through the centuries.

Admirers of Philip Larkin's 'Church-going' may think they recognize 'Some ruin-bibber, randy for antique, / Or Christmas-addict, counting on a whiff / Of gown-and-bands and organ-pipes and myrrh'. But Gordon Jackson is the author of *Spen River Anthology* (1982), which takes him and us back to his near-native country near Huddersfield, where churches count for less than chapels:

> They're selling off the chapels now –
> You can take your pick of two in Heckmondwike,
> There's the Free Methodist in the very centre
> Or High Street Upper Independent
> With a hyperbolic portico and graveyard.
> The churches, as redundant as the mills,
> Are peeling with recession, ignored
> As desecrated graves in their own churchyards . . .

And Jackson himself is an urchin of 'chapel', brought up – half-heartedly, he says – as a Baptist. Nor does he spurn High Street Upper Independent as a shabby travesty of York and Lincoln Minsters:

> I think its daft to call these mills
> dark and satanic. Just look at em,
> full o' winders, built like churches . . .
> . . . I think it's daft to call these mills
> dark and satanic: better call em
> Six-day chapels, and t' chapels Sabbath-mills.

When Jackson turns to translating the psalms – and there is a version of Psalm 50 in *Spen River Anthology*, along with a Nativity play where the shepherds speak West Riding dialect – the English of his own day that he looks for has traces of this spoken English of his childhood, the blunt and pithy English of Heckmondwike and Liversedge and Gomersal. In some ears from the Home Counties this may make his versions sound 'evangelical'; though this is largely an illusion created by his diction and his rhythms, it's an illusion that I think he might be quite happy with.

Jackson's versions are faithful, in the crucial sense that they are reverent. Though he is well aware of working in the aftermath of the modernist discovery, associated in English particularly with Ezra Pound, that the borderline between translation and adaptation is chimerical, he has chosen not to take advantage of the Poundian liberties that that perception legitimates. He made his position clear in the Introduction to his *Asgill Psalter* (1992):

> Without departing from the awesome authority of Coverdale, I have tried, by shifts of register, to repersonalize the matter, and by giving greater sway to the metaphors, and unity to the rhythm, to recover a feel of their essentially poetic character. I do this in all ignorance of Hebrew, and in great astonishment that no one seems to have done it before.

Now that Miles Coverdale's authority, as translator of the Psalms for use in public worship, has been shown to be a great deal less than 'awesome' – since after 450 years his versions are being superseded by those of David L. Frost, which have to be (Frost himself protesting) more respectful for instance of the 'inclusive' language demanded by feminists – Jackson's reverence for his great predecessor Coverdale comes over as conservative, not to say reactionary. But then the great modernists, Pound and Eliot among them, were nothing if not conservative. 'Make It New' was their cry; which is at the opposite extreme from 'Junk it, and start again'. Jackson's reverence is not just for Miles Coverdale, and for Holy Writ behind him; it is for 'the ancestors', whether they spoke West Riding English or Estuary English. They were not necessarily wiser than we are; they were at least as wise. And their wisdom, which goes back to ancient Israel, is what Gordon Jackson, with hard brush and cleaning fluid, aims to preserve. I know of no other man of letters in England who has aimed so high.

DONALD DAVIE